D1260410

ARGUMENTATION AND DEBATE: Taking the Next Step

TEACHER'S AND COACH'S GUIDE

ARGUMENTATION AND DEBATE: Taking the Next Step

TEACHER'S AND COACH'S GUIDE

Edited by Deborah Bush Haffey, Jeffrey B. Motter, and Christy L. Shipe

HOME SCHOOL LEGAL DEFENSE ASSOCIATION

Home School Legal Defense Association, Purcellville, Virginia 20132.

© 2004 by Dr. Deborah Bush Haffey, Jeffrey B. Motter, and Christy L. Shipe

ISBN 1-880665-01-8

www.hslda.org

Contents

APPENDIX

Acknowledgements

The editors wish to thank David H. Robey, Paula Bently, and Skip Rutledge for their contributions to this guide.

INTRODUCTION

How to Use This Book

by Christy L. Shipe

As the parent or coach of a student debater, you are seeking to train your young person in skills that will serve him for a lifetime. The material contained in this guide will help you do just that. The editors of *Argumentation and Debate: Taking the Next Step* have prepared several articles that will assist your overall efforts as a coach as well as unique material that will help you teach from the textbook either at home or in a class setting.

Coaching Tips is a compilation of resources for coaches and parents. Jeffery B. Motter and Deborah Bush Haffey combine their many years of coaching experience at Cedarville University to provide indispensable information for any debate coach or parent in "**Eight Coaching Tips**." Some of the tips are practical, such as caring for debaters at a tournament; others focus on teaching, such as using your meetings effectively; and still others address the spiritual aspects of debate, such as how to stay calm in the midst of controversy. This article will greatly aid your efforts to provide godly training for your students.

Paula Bently, a veteran debate mom and club leader from the National Christian Forensics and Communications Association (NCFCA), responds to common inquires in "**Addressing Questions Most Often Asked by New Debate Parents**." She helps coaches anticipate the issues that weigh on the minds of parents who are new to debate, such as the amount of time they should expect their student's involvement with debate to take each season.

In "**All I Really Needed to Know About Debate I Learned in Kindergarten**," Skip Rutledge takes a tongue-in-cheek look at some of the terminology surrounding the debate activity that can confuse parents and even coaches. Mr. Rutledge serves as the Director of Forensics at Point Loma University and will help you begin to decipher that "foreign" debate language your students suddenly begin speaking.

The *Chapter Outlines* present material that will supplement your understanding of the text and provide you with ideas for discussion questions and group or individual exercises. The outlines follow the exact structure of the textbook chapters, with a brief summary of the text, teacher's notes, suggestions for further study, discussion questions, and/or exercises at each point in the outline.

In the chapter outlines, the **teacher's notes** suggest ways to teach the text, important points to emphasize, or additional material that you may want to teach your student at that point of the text.

The suggestions **for further study** provide a jumping-off point for you to supplement the text with material from outside sources. Chapter 8, for instance, provides information for further study of the appropriate protocol for the questioning periods of cross-examination debate.

The **discussion questions** included in the chapter outlines can be used either in written form as homework assignments or for class discussion. If you are teaching a large class, you may want to use the questions you feel are most important as a homework assignment in order to give everyone the opportunity to answer. A suggested answer is included with each question so that you can accurately gauge your students' understanding of the question.

The authors of each chapter have also provided **exercises** that will help students understand and apply the chapter material in a concrete way. Many of these exercises can be done at home, although some are geared toward a classroom setting. Homeschooling parents should have no trouble adapting the exercises for individual students.

Finally, David H. Robey, Professor of Communications at Cedarville University, has contributed "**Team Activities**" to help a debate club develop into a unified team built upon trust and open communication.

As you use the material contained here and in the text, remember that it all means nothing if it is not based upon the truth of God. Smart people go wrong when they forget that everything they have comes from God and that everything they think must start with him. You will do your students a grave disservice if you allow them to believe that basing their thoughts or actions on "common sense" is enough. You and your students must *start* with God and build everything you believe from that foundation. If you start with common sense and then try to fit God into what you already believe, you will create a house built upon sand instead of a house built upon rock. It is the *foundation* of your thinking that is crucial; if the foundation is flawed, everything is flawed. But if you and your students begin your thinking and learning with God, then you will build upon a foundation that will last for eternity.

Scripture supports this idea when it says, "We demolish arguments and every pretension that sets itself up against the knowledge of God, and we take captive every thought to make it obedient to Christ" (II Corinthians 10:5, NIV). In order to demolish arguments, we must first make our thoughts obedient to Christ. Urge your students to found their thinking upon Christ, and when the opposition comes, they will be prepared to conquer every pretension that sets itself up against the knowledge of God.

Christy L. Shipe, author of An Introduction to Argumentation and Debate, *helped found the first debate league for homeschool students and now sits on the board of directors of the National Christian Forensics and Communications Association.*

COACHING TIPS

Eight Coaching Tips

by Deborah Bush Haffey and Jeffrey B. Motter

Tip 1: Coaching through conflict

Whether you are a debate coach, a parent, or both, remaining calm during conflict that involves your student can often be a challenge. We have all heard about parents involved in their children's competitive sports who became unreasonably angry with umpires or competitors. A few years ago, a father of a high school hockey player even killed another father. Though an extreme example, this situation illustrates the problems that arise when a parent's God-given desire to protect and promote his child rages out of control. Even coaches who are not parents feel a natural tie to their students. It is no easy thing to find the balance between guaranteeing that there is a level playing field for your own students and giving the other judges, coaches, and children the benefit of the doubt.

In striving to achieve the appropriate balance, it will be helpful for you to keep in mind that debate is a training ground and not an end in itself. According to Miriam Maddox, the founder of the debate program at Cedarville University, the purpose of teaching communication to Christian students is to create "communicators for Christ." As you coach debate in the midst of conflict, it will be very important to keep in focus that creating communicators for Christ—not winning—is your ultimate goal.

Nor is the debate round an indication of your ability as a parent or coach. Many wonderful, well-coached students lose debate rounds. In fact, the average debater will lose half his rounds! Winning and losing are simply normal processes of life. Until you are at peace with the fact that your student could lose every single round, and until you are completely satisfied with the goal of training students for Christ rather than winning, it would be best for you to excuse yourself and your student from participation in tournaments.

Of course, legitimate injustices do occur, and part of your job as the coach is to ensure that such injustices are curtailed. You must, however, take care to resolve each problem in a way that models "communicating for Christ." Here are some practical tips to make certain that your response advances that goal:

1. *Never* confront another person while you are too angry to display a Christ-like attitude. If you as the coach lose control of your emotions, you will set a bad example for your debaters and upset them in the process. The key to remaining calm is to yield yourself to Christ in the moment of conflict and realize that some matters, such as another debater's conduct or a judge's decision, are beyond your control. Unfavorable situations provide a wonderful opportunity for you to remind your students (and yourself!) that life isn't always easy or kind.

2. Seek to understand the situation before arriving at a judgment. Situations that seem unethical or unbiblical at first glance can usually be clarified as a mere misunderstanding or miscommunication.

3. Approach each situation with an attitude of "I might be wrong"—that is, with an attitude of giving the other person the benefit of the doubt.

4. *Never* confront another student; that is the job of his parent or coach. If you notice a student who has a problem, take your concerns to his parent or coach.

5. If you have a problem with a parent or a judge, go to that person—and no other—to resolve your differences. If you speak to others first or complain to others about unresolved conflict, you are guilty of the sin of gossip.

6. If the conflict cannot be settled with the other parent or coach, go to the tournament director. Remember that the tournament director's decision will stand as final for the day.

7. If you are not satisfied with the tournament director's decision, you can appeal to the NCFCA state representative.

We are emphasizing a godly response to conflict because we have witnessed countless occasions in which parents and coaches have engaged in childish disputes about winning. Your students are watching your behavior and learning from your reactions, for good or for ill. When the focus of debate becomes winning at all costs instead of the educational and spiritual skills that debate teaches, the whole activity is contaminated. The most valuable lesson you can teach your debaters is to engage in *godly* communication and behavior. Coaching through conflict is the perfect classroom for teaching this lesson.

Tip 2: Responding to debaters' complaints

It is not uncommon for debaters to come to their coaches during the course of a tournament to complain about their judges and opponents, either because they believe an injustice has occurred or because they are mirroring a complaint made by someone else. Do not allow your students to indulge such an attitude. When this predictable scenario occurs, *always* take the perspective of the other team in order to balance what your own students are saying. Remind your team that other students will sometimes make claims of "injustice" against them; when that happens your students probably won't realize they had done anything wrong, just as the students they are criticizing are probably unaware of a problem. Graciously ask questions of your students and of the appropriate officials, if necessary, that will help you gain a better understanding of what happened in the debate round. Most of the time what seems like a great "injustice" is a minor issue that had no real effect on the judge's decision.

Sometimes students will complain after they read their ballots from the tournament and conclude, "There is no possible way that we lost that round." Judges are certainly not infallible, yet debaters should be taught that the judge's decision should always be respected and accepted. Even inexperienced judges are able to follow arguments and be good critics of a debater's strengths and weaknesses. If a judge voted for the other team, it is usually because your students did not explain themselves clearly enough for the judge to vote for them. Simply encourage your students to learn from their losing ballots and see what areas need improvement. As ballots are consistently examined, it almost always becomes evident that there are recurring "themes" for each student that reveal areas he needs to work on.

If you find that one judge is consistently voting against your students, read his ballots carefully to determine what he expects. Write down on a piece of paper a summary of his expectations and give a copy to all your debaters, instructing them to adapt to that judge. There are always reasons the judge voted against your students, so be sure to take the opportunities that these "teachable moments" give. Almost all students learn more from a judge's comments on a losing ballot than on a winning one. Help your students realize that losing ballots, painful as they are, can be friends in disguise.

Again, the key is to give one another the benefit of the doubt. Assuming the best of people will help your students learn from their losses and make the debate tournament much more enjoyable and educational for everyone.

Tip 3: Coaching outrounds

Congratulations! Your team made it to the elimination rounds!

As a coach, stay calm. Now more than ever, you will need to refrain from the typical mistake of over-coaching your team. Even if your students beg you for guidance, avoid giving them "ten ways to defeat the other team" or they will get so caught up in the details of what you said that they will forget to do the things that got them to the outrounds in the first place.

Instead of frantic suggestions, simply remind your students of three calming facts: (1) that they made it to the outrounds in the same way as their opponents— by arguing a good case well; (2) that this is just another round, no different in style or structure from the rounds they have successfully completed; and (3) that this new round, like all others, will be won by sticking to the basics: evidence, stock issues, and refutation.

Remember, your team is there because it is good. Your students made it to the elimination rounds on their own merit and will have a good debate regardless of what you tell them at this point. Now is the time to relax and enjoy the debate.

Tip 4: Pairing teams

There is no exact science to pairing teams, but following these principles will give you a place to start when it comes time to pair students:

1. After you have had a chance to hear the students speak, identify those students who are comfortable responding immediately to an argument and those students who need time to process arguments. "Quick thinkers" are usually the ones who ask a lot of questions in class; "processors" are usually better at seeing how all of the little arguments fit into the larger whole. Pairing a quick thinker with a processor is a complementary combination and creates a team that can cover a broad range of arguments and styles from either an affirmative or negative perspective.

2. When you are deciding speaker order *on the negative*, the first speaker should be the one who thinks most quickly. Usually, a quick thinker is also a detail-oriented person, easily able to go straight down the affirmative case point-by-point. The second negative speaker hears three speeches before his second negative constructive (2NC), allowing him to process how all the specific points raised in the first negative constructive (1NC) fit together. This speaker should therefore be the one who is best able to take the "big picture" approach, fitting all of the little arguments into the larger whole.

3. When you are deciding speaker order *on the affirmative*, consider which team member is most familiar with the case. The second affirmative speaker must respond to all of the first negative speaker's arguments, so it is best to have the person most familiar with the case—whether a quick thinker or a processor— fill that role. Although it is important that the person presenting the first

affirmative constructive (1AC) be familiar with the case as well, make sure that the "expert" goes second.

Tip 5: Coaching difficult teams

Difficult-to-work-with debaters are not hard to spot! These are the students who balk at the suggestions of others, withhold evidence to gain personal advantage at the tournament, argue on the basis of what they think will win rather than on the basis of truth, and become upset at judges or opponents when they lose. Worse yet, their prideful spirit sometimes infects teammates, creating uncoachable teams.

When faced with such a debater or team, it will be important for you to graciously emphasize that everyone earns a position on the team: no debater is indispensable. In order to remain on the team, each student must be willing to contribute to the team, be considerate of others in the club, and listen to his coach (Philippians 2:3–4). Of course, you are not always right and teams don't need to run every argument that you like, but students must be willing to listen to you and work out their differences with you, or the issue will need to be raised with the debater and his parents. If problems continue after that, there comes a time when you will need to let the student go, because you simply cannot coach students who won't allow you to be the coach. Though it is difficult to set firm boundaries, removing an uncoachable student from the team may be the best thing both for the debater himself and for the rest of the group.

A prideful team can sometimes be turned around by simply allowing the students to lose. Rather than repeating attempts to coach the team and change what the students are doing wrong, you can allow them to do what they think is best and reap the consequences at tournaments. Losing ballots have a way of humbling one's pride.

A few years ago, we coached a team with one particular member who would not listen to us or to her partner. Every time her partner would suggest something, she would just tell him it wouldn't work and move on. Needless to say, her frustrated partner started doing his own thing in the round. Because they were not working together as a team, they ended up making completely different arguments in the round.

It goes without saying that they did not do well at their first tournament. At the time, we were unaware of what was occurring between them and just assumed that this team happened to have a bad tournament; after all, even the best teams have bad tournaments. We read the ballots, but nothing of significance concerned us. After a second tournament with a losing record, we started wondering what was going on.

We began to sit in on their rounds and noticed that one team member was doing things that were the exact opposite of what we had recommended. Even though we told her the reason she was losing was because of one specific weak argument, she continued to do "what she thought was best." After a while, we just stopped trying to coach her and allowed her and her unfortunate partner to continue to lose.

At the tournament before Nationals, she approached us and asked, "I win first speaker at every tournament, but we never have a winning record. What am I doing wrong?" She was so frustrated that they had been doing poorly the entire year that she finally came to her coaches asking for help. We proceeded to tell her that she was losing because she wasn't listening to her partner or her coaches. This realization came as quite a shock to her, and she immediately began listening to us. At the next tournament, which was Nationals, the team won. Sometimes letting a team do its own thing for awhile teaches debaters that if they aren't going to listen to the opinions of others, they will lose. The debater in this example still thanks us for this difficult but valuable lesson.

Tip 6: Caring for debaters at tournaments

Coaches who have themselves debated fully realize how draining a debate tournament is for the debaters. If you haven't competed in a debate tournament, though, it may be difficult to imagine the mental and physical exhaustion debaters experience. One debate round lasts as long as half of a basketball game, so in essence debaters "play" three games in just the preliminary rounds. The intense intellectual gymnastics of this sport leave players mentally depleted and physically exhausted.

Meeting your debaters' intellectual and emotional needs at tournaments is always a tricky thing. You want to give your debaters enough space to feel that they have the freedom to work out problems on their own, yet at the same time let them know that they can come to you with any questions.

If you have a beginning team, it is essential that you make yourself available to your students between rounds so that that they can clarify questions as they go. Share whatever knowledge you have about the teams and judges they will face. If you know their opponent's affirmative case or how the opponent likes to argue on the negative, let your students know before they face that team. If you know the judge's philosophy, help them understand it so that they can adapt to their audience. Keep in mind that the biggest learning curve for new debaters comes within the first four tournaments, so you will want to be the most available to them then.

Experienced teams generally like more space to solve problems. The best time to talk with your experienced debaters may be at night or during a meal. Simply asking "How do you think things are going?" and "How is your affirmative case working?" will usually be enough to start them talking about what has happened in their debate rounds up to that point.

The two most helpful things that you as a coach can do to ease the physical strain are to help keep the tournaments running on time and to provide adequate food and rest for your debaters. Bring snacks and water to help debaters get through the day, especially for rounds that may go past the dinner hour. Also, it is wise to bring some medication that will alleviate headaches, although headaches can often be avoided if debaters are properly nourished and hydrated.

Of course, one of the best things for you to do in caring for your debaters is to pray with them and for them, both before and during tournaments. Prayer helps remind them why they are involved in academic debate and that, first and foremost, all the glory belongs to God. Keeping the focus fixed on God makes the frustrating things at a tournament seem insignificant.

Tip 7: Running a debate meeting

Familiarity with some general guidelines about what to cover in your meetings as the season progresses will help make each meeting as beneficial as possible.

Before the first meeting

Spend several hours preparing your own research in order to identify four to six central topics that can be the starting point for class discussion and research. As you personally research the resolution, take note of topics that seem to come up frequently. Those recurring topics will serve as the foundation of your first official meeting.

The first meeting

Most affirmative cases will be based on one of the main topic areas you have already identified, so these should be the first areas you research. To keep debaters from feeling overwhelmed, keep all discussion focused on these areas. If a student wants to delve into more obscure research, tell him, "That's a very interesting area that we will need to research in a few weeks." For now, insist that the group stay focused. Based on the topic areas you have chosen, you should use the first meeting to assign students different research responsibilities. Dividing the research areas among students will allow you to cover a lot of ground in a short amount of time. Have each person prepare a one-page summary of the research he finds, to be presented at the next meeting. Point out that by dividing, your students can conquer.

It is also essential that you begin preliminary discussion of the resolution at this first meeting by considering its wording, discussing its social context, and analyzing the extent to which it is true. Discussion of the resolution will continue for several months as debaters research and refine their ideas, but spend as much time as you can at this first meeting getting your debaters started.

▶Wording

▷ From this first meeting, make it a habit to always *use the exact wording of the resolution* as you discuss and research the topic. Affirmatives must affirm *exactly* what the resolution requires, nothing more, nothing less.

▷ Understand the terms as they are used within the context of the resolution, then define each resolutional term in a manner that is consistent with the topic as a whole. Pay special attention to modifiers such as *substantial* and *significant.* NCFCA rules are written to prevent affirmatives from defining terms in a way that violates a common-sense understanding of the intent of the resolution, so keep your students focused on reasonable definitions.

▷ Identify the action required by or the controversy contained within the resolution. Policy cases will require affirmatives to take a specific action; value cases require teams to discuss a conflict of values.

▶Social context

▷ A broad base of knowledge about the subject area of the resolution will be an invaluable resource in the debate round. In order to appreciate why the topic of the resolution is important, grasp the cultural and historical significance of the topic area, and discern the key issues involved, students must be encouraged to read as much as they can about the topic. Perhaps at this first meeting you could help your students begin researching current events that relate to some aspect of the resolution, pointing out the relationship between an informed citizenry and a free society.

▷ Have students examine the societal problem that the resolution addresses by answering the questions *What is the big deal? How does it affect the people in my town?* and *Who cares?* These common questions which we all ask of issues in society are actually another form of the stock issues of debate.

▷ By the time they have five articles, students need to begin organizing and dividing their material. Otherwise, the amount of information can overwhelm them. In later meetings, after students have gathered enough information, help them examine the resolution to separate those issues that fall on affirmative ground from those that fall on negative ground.

▶Analysis

▷ Help your students analyze both the breadth of research necessary for their cases and which research areas each debater should cover. This choice is an individual one that students will make (with your help) according to their particular case topic area and potential negative strategies. Again, all teams should at least have enough background information to talk relatively knowledgeably about the topic.

▷ This is where the fun begins! Having carefully researched the topic, students should now analyze the extent to which the resolution is true or false. Debaters must also be able to address the positive and the negative aspects of the resolution. Addressing these aspects after researching the topic helps students learn to withhold judgment until they have a full understanding of the issue. Then, when they take a position on this controversial subject, they will be able to give well-supported reasons for why they think the way they do.

The second and subsequent meetings

Begin these meetings by having students present their one-page summaries of the particular research topic each was assigned. After they have heard the preliminary research, have the group brainstorm potential case ideas. Continue with your evaluation of the resolution—its wording, its social context, and the stand your students take on it. At the conclusion of your discussion, determine research topics again and divide those assignments up among the students for presentation at the next meeting.

After your first tournament

After your team has attended a tournament, your meetings will primarily consist of finding out what evidence gaps your debaters have and patching up their affirmative cases. Make sure to have your debaters bring their flow sheets from the last tournament to the meeting to help them remember which of their own arguments lacked sufficient evidence and what successful arguments other teams were making.

If you find that your debaters are especially good at flowing, ask them to write down the source citation of the other team's evidence at the next tournament. Having citations will allow them to go home and find an article that they suspect another team is misusing. If the opposition was indeed misusing evidence, your students can "pin them to the wall" at the next tournament. Unfortunately, cheaters sometimes win. The best way to stop this unfair practice is often to show them through careful research that cheating doesn't pay off in the end. Once a team is caught cheating, its credibility is undermined for its entire debate career.

At these after-tournament meetings, you should also review the ballots with your debaters. Highlight areas that need improvement. Specifically discuss arguments that were being explained well and arguments that were not. Good arguments don't lose because the judge is inexperienced; rather, good arguments lose because the debater didn't explain herself well enough. Reviewing the ballots with your team will let everyone see what she can do to improve.

Practice debates

Holding practice debates during your meetings can be a very beneficial exercise for your students but is also incredibly time-consuming. Plan on taking at least two-and-a-half hours for each debate: an hour and a half for the practice round itself and an additional hour for extensive coaching after the practice round ends. The time involved may seem excessive, but what your students learn from actually debating and then receiving immediate feedback will be well worth the investment.

Tip 8: Researching the topic

Many parents and coaches make the mistake of thinking that they must know more about the topic than their students. Please rest assured that you are not expected to be an encyclopedia of knowledge about the topic. Rather, it is the job of your debaters to research and know the topic very well.

In fact, after months spent researching the resolution, debaters often know so much about the topic that they cannot see if a line of reasoning makes sense, particularly if they are assuming something in their arguments that a lay judge with very little knowledge of the topic will not understand. That's where you come in. Because you are distanced from intimate knowledge of the topic, you will be able to see your debaters' arguments from the judge's perspective and offer better advice than if you knew every detail of their research. Simply critique, ask questions, and offer suggestions.

In short, the best debaters know how to take complicated, detailed information and communicate it clearly to an audience of average adults; the best coaches are "average adults."

Deborah Bush Haffey, Ph.D., is Associate Professor of Communication Arts at Cedarville University, where she has served as the award-winning Director of Debate for 14 years.

Jeffrey B. Motter, Ph.D. candidate, served as Instructor of Communication Arts and Director of Debate at Cedarville University from 2001–2003, receiving awards both as a debater and as a coach.

Addressing Questions Most Often Asked by New Debate Parents

by Paula Bently

At the beginning of each debate season, I hold a mandatory parent meeting for new families who are interested in joining our club. From those meetings I have come to realize that nearly all parents who are new to debate have particular questions that weigh on their minds. It is from those questions that this article is born.

As you "listen in" on our questions and answers, please keep in mind that I coach homeschool debaters who compete in the NCFCA. Therefore, some of the answers are reflections of, but are certainly not limited to, that particular league. Even if your team does not participate in the NCFCA, you should nevertheless find our 'parents' meeting" helpful as you seek to address the questions most commonly asked by parents whose children are first-time debaters.

Question 1: What will debate do for my children spiritually?

Consider the instructions that Paul gave young Timothy, who was probably not much older when he received Paul's letter than some of our own young people involved with debate: "Don't let anyone look down on you because you are young, but set an example for the believers in speech, in life, in love, in faith, and in purity. . . . Watch your life and doctrine closely. Persevere in them, because if you do, you will save both yourself and your hearers" (I Timothy 4:12–16, NIV).

Above all else, debate is an exercise in exemplary speech—a sound message passionately delivered with thoughtfully chosen words—and speech, you will note, is first on this God-breathed list. It stands to reason, then, that the kind of communication practiced by debaters is nothing short of a spiritual exercise.

Another spiritual discipline cultivated by debate is the habit of evaluating everything we read or hear. Remember the Bereans of Acts 17? Scripture tells us that the believers of this city "were of more noble character than the Thessalonians, for they received the message with great eagerness and examined the Scriptures every day to see if what Paul said was true" (Acts 17:11, NIV).

Because debate rewards a student for questioning everything she hears, your students will—like the Bereans—be encouraged to evaluate everything in life that same way! When she learns a new teaching, watches the news, or reads an article, her debate training will prompt her to be constantly asking herself questions: *Is the author verifying what he is saying, or is what I am reading the author's opinion? Is the author being consistent throughout the entire article? Is the point being made consistent with the author's source? Does it make sense logically? Are there logical fallacies in the point this person is trying to make? Can I read the original source and see if it's quoted within the correct context? Can I verify the source of the facts? How were those facts obtained?*

With all of the worldly and ungodly teachings today, many of which sound good initially, we want our young people to learn to properly question everything they hear. The more a student questions, the more solid will be his beliefs. Don't be afraid when your child begins to question what he believes. Make him search out the answers and watch as he becomes spiritually stronger. Honest analysis—the heart of successful debate—will lead him to the truth of sound doctrine.

There is yet a third spiritual exercise employed by debaters, and that is the opportunity for young people to "set an example" in the "life" of the debate round itself.

Several years ago, for instance, a debate coach from a different league came to judge at one of the Ohio tournaments. She was completely amazed not only at the level of skill the students possessed, but more importantly at the friendships the competitors had with each other. Because these students adopted the perspective that ". . . iron sharpens iron . . ." (Proverbs 27:17, NIV) and refused to view the opposing team as some sort of enemy, they made friends all over the country, often praying with competitors and even helping them with their cases! After observing this team, the visiting coach was determined to go back, change the way her club was run, and talk to those in authority about changing the attitudes of the competitors in her league. When the coach asked me why there was such a difference in this league, I had an opportunity to share the Gospel with her—a door that opened because of the exemplary behavior of young people. The debater does not need to wait until adulthood for his communication and critical thinking skills to impact his world.

What will debate do for a student spiritually? It will give him the tools to evaluate not only what he believes but why he believes it, then live out those beliefs "in speech" and "in life" with the disciplined emotion and careful patience that will enable a lost world to hear. What more could a parent ask for?

Question 2: What will debate do for my children academically?

I do not know of a single subject that offers a broader education or more life skills than debate. Whatever the resolution, a student will almost certainly cover government, economics, political science, composition, research, public speaking, logic, rhetoric, current events, typing/word processing, computer skills, editing, and argumentation and debate theory as she prepares for the debate. Depending upon the topic, a student in the process of doing research may also study certain sciences, geography, a segment of history, and/or the founding documents of our country. She must organize her time to complete tasks, discipline herself to refute and rebuild arguments within the strict time limits of the debate round, and learn to appreciate the unique personalities of her teammates—life skills that are viable in any profession.

The knowledge and skills gained through debate can easily be documented on a high school transcript, validating the academic value of this discipline. You may format the transcript one of two ways: The first option is to arrange the credits by year to reflect what studies were done the freshman year, what studies were done the sophomore year, etc. The second option is to arrange the credits by subject. I find this option more advantageous since most participants debate for several years. Thus, subjects that did not get a full credit's worth of time in one year can be credited on the basis of the cumulative time spent.

Whichever transcript option you choose, you will need to keep a general record of the time your student spends on debate. Of course, there will be some weeks when your child spends more hours on debate and some weeks when he spends fewer, so I suggest you record an average amount of time spent rather than tediously logging every hour and what the student did during that hour.

Because of the large variety of subjects covered, you may choose to view debate not as a single academic subject nor as an extracurricular activity but rather as a unit study. As with all unit studies, the time spent needs to be reported in a way that colleges or universities can understand. Hence, the time spent will need to be divided into credit hours or Carnegie Units. According to the admissions office of Cedarville University, for example, 150 hours of instruction is one Carnegie Unit. Before writing a high school transcript, call the institution your child is hoping to attend, ask what a Carnegie Unit is based upon and how that institution determines grade point averages, then use the appropriate formula when preparing the transcript. The way different states and institutions track credit hours or Carnegie Units varies, but you may find the following general formula helpful:

Hours per week x number of weeks x number of years[*]
÷ the number of hours in a credit = number of credits given

10 hours per week x 30 weeks x 3 years
÷ 150 hours per credit = 6 credits (or Carnegie Units)

Once you have determined the time spent on debate and translated that time into the system used by your student's college of choice, you will need to divide those credits up among the various subject areas covered. Time spent on debate that did not equal a full credit can be combined with time spent on another activity within the same subject. As an illustration, consider the subject of civics: some of the student's time could have been spent during debate, but some of it could have been spent reading newsmagazines, volunteering in the community, or doing curriculum-based work.

Six credit hours of debate might be divided up as follows:
.50 credits for government
.50 credits for economics
.50 credits for civics
.50 credits for composition
.25 credits for public speaking
.50 credits for logic
.25 credits for current events
.25 credits for typing
.25 credits for computer skills
1.75 credits for argumentation and debate theory
.25 credits for "Agricultural Studies" (topic specific)
.25 credits for "Immigration Studies" (topic specific)
.25 credits for "Tax Reform" (topic specific)
6.00 total credits

Question 3: How much time will my child spend on debate?

Like every worthwhile activity, debate takes a sizable investment of time and energy. The time spent in debate will include, but is not limited to, attending club meetings, writing and researching cases, competing in tournaments, and participating in workshops. The club meetings generally range from one to two hours per week during a

---

[*] If formulating the transcript by year, then including "number of years" in the formula is obviously unnecessary.

calendar school year. Writing and researching cases is another time consideration. Some students write one case and argue it all year long; other students write new cases for every tournament they attend. Research can be a year-long project, averaging four hours per week. The tournaments are generally a day and a half long, not including travel time. Workshops—often presented by colleges during the summer— offer a place to help families get started with debate and provide an opportunity for students who do not have the luxury of a club to gather and share ideas. Additional time is required for individual coaching, meeting with a partner if participating in team debate, and attending practice meets or Round Robins. (See Question 8.)

To some extent, the time required will depend upon the level of involvement that you and your student decide upon. If your child plans to participate, she must spend time writing and researching cases, but it is not necessary, for example, to debate every weekend or attend every tournament; similarly, it is very helpful to attend the workshops, but not mandatory.

To help project the level of involvement that will be appropriate for your student, consider ahead of time that child's goals and personality. In fact, at the start of each year, ask him to write out his goals for that year and what he hopes to accomplish in debate. Typical goals for a new debater are "I want to be a better speaker" or "I want to learn how to properly refute an argument." The student who wants to improve his speaking will spend a greater portion of his time speaking in front of the mirror or an audience for critiques; the one who wants to learn how to refute an argument will invest more time learning debate refutation theory and analyzing opponents' cases. An advanced debater's goal might be to qualify for the National Tournament, requiring more time spent attending various tournaments and even out-of-state travel. Consider also your student's personality: if your child is very competitive, be prepared to allot more time to debate.

Again, there is no avoiding the fact that debate is going to require your child to invest sizeable portions of time. Just be careful to help her "dive in" thoughtfully so she can enjoy making new friends and having fun without burning out, exasperating the rest of the family, or depleting your family finances.

Question 4: How much time will we as parents spend on debate?

Debate is a family affair. On the one hand, the amount of time your student spends will be limited by how much time you are willing and able to give; on the other hand, the amount of time your student's involvement with debate costs you will be proportional to his level of involvement. For that reason, it will be very important for you and your student to openly discuss goals and limitations—both yours and his—at the beginning of each debate season. Some families make it their goal to involve their children in debate until the spiritual principles and academic skills the students should learn are used consistently in everyday life. For these parents, it doesn't matter how much time debate takes. However, for those families who have an older child in debate while trying to school and care for several younger siblings, time can be the ultimate decision maker.

Unless your student drives, it will be club meetings, tournaments, and traveling to and from those events that will demand the bulk of your "debate time." The time spent traveling to club meetings can often be curbed with carpooling. If not, find out from your local club how often and how long they meet, then consider that amount of time in addition to the amount of time it takes to travel to the club location. Our group has found having club meetings every other week to be of help to those families who don't live locally, making it a little easier on their schedules.

You must also factor in tournaments—traveling to and from the event as well as the time for the tournament itself. While there, please don't expect to sit back and watch the rounds. (For that, bring a friend with a video camera.) Rather, attend with the expectation of helping. Tournaments are run by volunteers, and every well-run tournament needs many volunteers with a wide variety of gifts and talents.

To start with, every debate parent should learn to judge. There are not many tournaments where all the judges are provided. Thus, if your child is involved, you will either have to learn how to judge or bring someone to judge for you. Rest assured that anyone who can make a decision can be a judge. For example, when you vote in an election, you cast a ballot for a candidate whether or not you under-stand all of the details and intricacies of the policies for which the candidate stands. Your decision is based on what has been communicated by that candidate. It is unnecessary for you to understand the full budget of Social Security to decide whether a candidate is moving in a direction that is illogical or lacks good sense. Likewise, it is unnecessary to completely understand debate theory in order to justify a decision. A decision is based upon communication within the round and whether it makes logical sense or not. Most parents find that they really enjoy the intellectual challenge of judging and the opportunity to encourage the debaters. (Besides, it's the only time you can't be wrong!) Judge orientations and workshops can help an apprehensive parent understand the rules of debate. Judging doesn't require any more time than attending the tournaments.

Other gifts and talents are needed, too. For instance, the gift of serving is especially helpful when working at the welcome table or in the judges' hospitality room, making food for the community judges. Skill with computers is necessary to help run the tabulation programs. The Tournament Director or Facility Coordinator needs volunteers who have the gift of administration. The list goes on. Contact the Tournament Director of the upcoming tournament you plan to attend and find out what volunteers are needed. The director will love you for it!

Question 5: How much will debate cost?

Numerous variables make it impossible for any coach to give an exact figure. Each family must consider various costs involved in debate—both mandatory and optional—and then reach its own bottom-line conclusion.

Costs that cannot be avoided include registration fees, league membership fees, office supplies, and fulfillment of the dress code. The registration fees for a tournament can range on average from $10.00 for a local practice meet to $30.00 or more for a qualifying tournament. If your child plans to attend the National Tournament, membership in the national league is mandatory. Fees and membership information for NCFCA can be found at www.ncfca.org.

Office supplies might include legal pads, sticky notes, pens and pencils, highlighters, a notebook or file box to organize the research, and other things to help your child organize his materials. The cost of photocopying research should also be factored in.

In addition, NCFCA has a mandatory dress code. While it is not necessary to have a new outfit or shirt and tie for each event, it may be necessary to buy your debater at least one new outfit or suit. It goes without saying that a little creativity can help keep this unavoidable expense to a minimum. If the dress code seems strict or financially burdensome, keep in mind that dress is the first form of communication. Appearance says something immediately about a person and what she stands for. Hopefully, outside of the debate rounds, your child will appreciate the importance of first impressions and not take her appearance lightly.

Some of the optional costs may include seminars or workshops, club or coaching fees, working with a partner, and traveling. The seminars and workshops can range from $20.00 for a guest speaker to several hundred dollars for college-level courses on debate theory. Club fees per year can range from $30.00 if the club is just getting started, to $500.00 per year for an experienced coach. Depending upon where the club is meeting, there may also be facility fees.

Working with a partner, especially an out-of-town partner, can mean money for travel and long-distance phone calls. If a partner lives out of town, email and

Instant Messenger are great ways to help defray these expenses. A lot of debate work can be done very economically using these tools.

Travel costs can include gasoline, normal vehicle wear and tear, eating out, and hotels. The variance, of course, is highly dependent on the location of the tournament in relation to where you live. Carpooling is very helpful in this respect. Also, it is not necessary to buy the meals offered at the tournament or to eat out while on the road because most tournaments offer a cafeteria where coolers can be stored. Some of them even have kitchens available with microwaves and outlets for crock pots. Ask the local Tournament Director what is available. Another cost saver is host housing where local families open their homes to those who are traveling. Availing yourself of host housing can greatly reduce lodging expenses and provide an opportunity to get to know other families from around the country. In return, you might consider offering your own home to an out-of-town debater, keeping in mind that the recipients of this kind gesture won't complain if your home doesn't look like a photo from *Better Homes and Gardens* or isn't better furnished than the Joneses'.

To help defray some of the costs of participating in debate, some families have done fundraising: selling candy bars door-to-door, offering meals at the local tournaments for a fee, etc. You shouldn't be afraid to have your son or daughter help out with the extra expenses, either. For one thing, bearing some personal responsibility might add a new dimension to the idea your child has about how many tournaments he attends. Furthermore, the competitor generally works harder for a self-earned tournament, so it may actually benefit your student's performance in the debate round to participate in raising money for the expenses of debate.

Question 6: How can we expect debaters to argue both sides of an issue?

In debate, a student is forced to examine issues from all angles in anticipation of the arguments that will be made against her case in order to be prepared with convincing answers. She does not necessarily need to *agree* with both sides, but must understand the issues involved so thoroughly that she can argue on behalf of either viewpoint.

The book of Proverbs affirms that to examine multiple viewpoints is to embrace wisdom, warning that "the first to present his case seems right, till another comes forward and questions him" (Proverbs 18:17, NIV). In other words, before anyone can truly make a sound decision or make a case for one side of an issue, he must first understand the other viewpoint(s) involved. To do so is to honor this principle of Scripture.

Of course, the real goal is for these principles of debate to carry over into real-life situations. Hopefully, learning to study all aspects of an issue thoroughly enough to argue from either side will encourage debaters to withhold their opinions until *after* a thorough investigation of both sides has been completed. Now doesn't that sound like a breath of fresh air!

Question 7: Why do you make students learn debate theory and then find inexperienced judges?

Again, debate should always be a learning tool for what your child will face in real life. Outside of the debate round, people with whom your child comes in contact will not necessarily be educated on the topic about which she is speaking. For instance, she will most likely be communicating Christ to people in this world who are unfamiliar with Christianity. As preparation for life, then, it is valuable for the debater to learn to communicate in such a way that the layperson—the person who knows nothing of the theory—feels like he or she just learned something and is now empowered to make a decision on the given topic. To effectively persuade a layperson, the student must employ every shred of debate theory that she knows, thinking through what she is trying to communicate so she can verbalize it convincingly. In contrast, she might be tempted to employ debate jargon and allow her debate theory to take the place of good delivery when arguing before a trained judge such as a debate coah. Though impressive, throwing around debate language and the rules and regulations of debate theory will not help train her to communicate to an average audience. In other words, then, lay judges provide a unique perspective that is highly valuable for training young people to persuade a mass audience.

It is true, of course, that a completely untrained judge is sometimes more easily persuaded by a persuasive but meaningless argument. Though unfortunate, delivery sometimes overshadows sound logic and good content. Some politicians, for example, have such a polished speaking style that their lack of content is overlooked and accepted. Our goal in training a judge with orientations and workshops is to help avoid this situation.

Regardless of the judge's training or experience, students must be taught to understand that the judge is always right. His decision cannot be changed. A debater should therefore never be allowed to criticize a judge or a judge's decision. If a competitor chooses to criticize a judge for an "unfair" loss, that debater should also be willing to admit when an undeserved win has been awarded—and I have yet to hear anyone complain about that or be willing to relinquish the round he shouldn't have won!

It will be easier for you and your student to accept the decisions of both experienced and inexperienced judges if you keep the focus of each round where it belongs: on learning to communicate well, on practicing life skills, and most of all on pleasing Christ. In short, trophies are carrots used to train students for real-life performance, not the ultimate goal. To make an issue of a judge's experience or a judge's decision is almost always to engage in carrot-worship.

Question 8: How do we start a club?

Starting a new club can be invigorating and frustrating at the same time, but the rewards are worth it.

First, network with other families.

Networking is a great way to get a club started. Many families, like yours, are also just exploring debate, some perhaps even locally. Other families have been involved for a while and remember what it was like when first attempting to start a club; you may be able to glean from their experiences.

To network with NCFCA families, go to www.ncfca.org and click on the link labeled "Local Contacts." Under that heading is the list of Regional Directors and State Representatives. If there is no State Representative for your state, contact your Regional Director. Ask for resources to help you start your own club.

You may want to get on the NCFCA email loop via the website and local email loops. (Email loops are group mailings which get passed from one group to another, often advertising seminars, workshops, conferences, tournaments, and other events of interest.) The NCFCA State Representative or Regional Director should be able to help with the local email loop and/or contact persons.

The following suggestions may help as you endeavor to pioneer a club in your area:

1. Contact the local representative of your state homeschool group to begin advertising that there is an interest in working with other families interested in learning argumentation and debate. Homeschool state organizations can be found through Home School Legal Defense Association at www.hslda.org.
2. Ask the NCFCA Regional Director or State Representative to send out an email with the same advertisement.
3. Advertise your desire to locate other families with an interest in debate in the local newspaper, in homeschool support group newsletters, and in church bulletins.

4. Sponsor a workshop or conference close to home in order to drum up interest.

5. Attend as many practice meets, tournaments, or other events as possible to meet families from your area who share your interest in starting a new debate club.

With a little perseverance you should easily find at least one or two other families who show an interest. Let me encourage you to be content with even a small network to start with. Most large clubs started with only a few families, and most clubs are still relatively small. It is almost certain that you will not be alone for long.

Second, join with your students in learning debate theory.

Taking the Next Step is obviously a great place to start. There are numerous other avenues to help with this task. For example, colleges and universities such as Cedarville University, Patrick Henry College, Bob Jones University, and Gutenberg College host summer debate camps and classes. Local seminars, workshops, and conferences also help teach debate theory. Consult your state homeschooling organization or NCFCA to learn about other opportunities.

Third, know the rules.

Once you have tackled debate theory, you will want to attend a practice meet or tournament to see how that knowledge is put to work in an actual debate round. Before attending, though, I highly recommend that you read the rules of the league. There may be some nuances that are different from other leagues or from the books you have read, such as the dress code or the stock issues. You are responsible to know the competition rules, so read them carefully.

Finally, partner students into complementary teams.

Once a club has been started and the students are ready to be partnered, I recommend that the coach or leader partner them. When students are left to choose their own partners, two popular students or the ones with the most trophies usually choose one another, leaving others out. Or, a student may have a tendency to stay in her comfort zone and pick her best friend. When that happens, either not much work gets done (despite the fact that these students spent every day together last week!) or the debaters aren't friends by the end of the year.

Having a coach or leader partner the debaters while bathing the decision in prayer is the best way. Put students together who complement each other. The best teammates are almost always students who are opposites in qualities but equals in abilities. Keep in mind that Lincoln-Douglas (LD) non-policy debate is a wonderful learning experience for individual students and is also available in the NCFCA league.

Conclusion

As with anything worthwhile that is done well, debate requires extensive time and resources. Most families, though, find that the benefits far outweigh any apprehensions they might have. Debate is an opportunity to prepare the next generation of leaders for the future and enable them to begin making a difference while they are young.

Paula Bently is a homeschooling mom and leader of debate for the Alpha-Omega Speech and Debate Association in Columbus, Ohio.

All I Really Needed to Know About Debate I Learned in Kindergarten:
A Coach's Guide to Encouraging Novice Debaters

by Skip Rutledge

With apologies to Jacques Derrida,* the following is an attempt (with tongue firmly planted in cheek) to deconstruct the intimidating and exclusionary lexicon of scholastic debate that contributes heavily to novice flight. The purpose is to invite and encourage greater participation among those instructors, coaches, and students who might otherwise feel linguistically marginalized. To ease this transition, a brief "kidspeak" jargon-to-slang primer will be provided.

An Invitation to New Debaters and Coaches

Please do not get too discouraged. Debate really is fun. Admittedly, there are growing numbers of detractors pining for the good old days, when every inconsequential argument did not immediately invite twelve independent links leading to the thermonuclear destruction of the planet at the hands of psycho-narco-feminist-skinhead terrorists. Notwithstanding such objections, debate is still an exciting, intellectually stimulating way to engage bright young minds in a game that sharpens participants' skills in critical thinking and analysis, public speaking, research, writing, and listening. Additionally, the game of debate teaches all the participants (coaches, judges, competitors, and observers alike) the importance of staying well-versed in both national and international current affairs.

But there are several significant barriers facing beginning debaters and coaches in scholastic debate. For one thing, beginning debaters are easily intimidated by the

---

* Jacques Derrida (1930–) French philosopher celebrated as the principal exponent of deconstructionism, a term he coined for the critical examination of the fundamental conceptual distinctions, or "oppositions," inherent in Western philosophy since the time of the ancient Greeks. (Jacques Derrida. Encyclopædia Britannica. 2004. Encyclopædia Britannica Online. 2 Aug. 2004 <http://search.eb.com/eb/article?eu=30509>.)

hyper-speed of delivery present in most college leagues. They are not able to under-stand what other debaters are saying nor speak at such a speed themselves. Although the speed of delivery is not currently a problem in NCFCA, coaches and critics need to make a conversational delivery style a priority in order to prevent this problem in the not too distant future.

Another barrier, perhaps more unique to NCFCA debate, is the tendency to wage argumentation in terms of moral absolutes. Certain debaters seem unable to argue the relative merits of a value or policy without insisting that anyone who disagrees is of Satan. While this is a bit of an exaggeration to make my point, I have seen this demonization tactic used more times than I care to remember.

My chief concern, however, is the often incomprehensible jargon that permeates our activity. In coaching at the college level, I have found that the greatest chal-lenge in developing a debate squad is encouraging new debaters to stay with the activity after they watch a "real" debate round. It would be wonderful to be able to show these eager beginners a dialectical contest of eloquent orators demonstrating the polish and wit often showcased in the formerly televised *Firing Line* debates by William F. Buckley and friends. Instead, as a coach of novices, I spend most of my time translating what technical terms I can actually recognize to overwhelmed beginners observing a debate round.

And in spite of my years of experience, I sometimes find myself guessing at words to go with the letters to which debaters typically reduce technical phrases of two or more utterances. All too often, the debater is reading someone else's briefs and is not quite clear on what is meant. The logical fallacy of hasty generalization becomes "hasty G" and topicality becomes "T." Weapons of mass destruction become simply "WMD." Not surprisingly, most of my observing beginners disappear, since they just wanted to debate, not endure learning a complex new language.

It is likely that debaters will always collect and display new or bizarre terms as if they were merit badges that hierarchically elevate "enlightened debaters" above the uninformed masses. For example, when confronted with a policy proposal one would rather not specifically debate, why not instead debate its deontological aspects or its postmodern ramifications, especially if the opposition does not fully understand deontology or postmodernism?

In spite of the complicated jargon some debaters insist on using to communicate their arguments, please know that it is possible for novice coaches and beginning debaters alike to easily teach and learn the fundamentals of debate. The technical terminology of this game need not be oppressive or exclusionary. Best-selling author Robert Fulghum contended that everything he really needed to know in life, he learned in kindergarten.* I would add, tongue in cheek, that most everything you really need to know about scholastic debate fundamentals you learned in kindergarten as well, just by different names.

The following is therefore intended to translate some of the more intimidating phrases of the current debate world into user-friendly terminology. It will further be shown that many of these concepts were widely employed on the playground between tricycle races, around the jungle gym set, or while socializing over graham crackers chased by healthy swigs of warm milk prior to nap time. The bottom line is not only that debate is fun but also that anyone who desires can enter into this activity. Beyond that, when confronted with an intimidating new term or phrase, merely try to relate it back to your kindergarten experiences. It will almost certainly find its origins there.

Kindergarten Arguments Revisited: A Primer

Most of the important lines of reasoning that scholastic debaters utilize can be categorized in the following lexicon of simplistic responses or queries: (1) *but why* whines, (2) *huh-uh* denials, (3) *so what* challenges, (4) *that's stupid* retorts, and the all-important (5) *hey, that's mine* claim. This simple terminology is not an attempt to denigrate or belittle the activity of debate in any way, but merely to throw open wide its linguistic doors, which may have been barring admittance to many of the marginalized.

1. The "but why" whine

Anyone with a memory of his own childhood, or anyone who has spent time with children recently, can confirm that one of children's most annoying tendencies is their unending fascination with playing the *but why* game. No matter how simple or complex the answer given, it is always met with a *but why* challenge. In desperation, the parent will finally declare, "Because I said so!" It is true that this response

---

* This attempt to demystify terminology may well be met with disfavor in certain academic circles. It is hoped that the more scholastically inclined within the community will recognize the intended purpose and tone, rather than take offense. This approach is in no way intended to demean the serious academic pursuits in developing the various argumentation concepts alluded to herein. Neither should the reader confuse the proposed parallel "kidspeak" terminology with the excellent insights reported by Meyer (1992) regarding preschoolers and argumentative power, O'Keefe and Benoit (1982) regarding children's arguments, Reike and Willbrand (1986) regarding reason giving in children's supplicatory compliance gaining, and van Eemersen, et al, (1995) regarding Dutch secondary education students and unexpressed argumentative premises.

can be useful when parents are attempting to teach the importance of respecting authority. In fact, Christian comedian Jeff Allen has a routine about how silly it would be to debate the subtler nuances of cause-and-effect reasoning with an eighteen-month-old infant who is about to place his tongue in an electric socket. But at a certain age, it is also good to provide strong reasons for behavior so that children will understand and appreciate the principles involved, in addition to the commands or rules. Absent the ability to discern good from bad reasoning, children run the future risk of becoming the unwitting pawns of others who will bear strong influence on their lives, such as peers, con artists, television celebrities, musicians, or movie producers.

Asking and answering the *but why* question either in the debate round or in life situations is a crucial part of developing critical thinking skills. In fact, there is no greater skill a critical thinker can develop than the ability to constantly ask himself, or his opponent in cross examination, "But why?" In the debate round, "because I said so" falls flat as a response when the respondent is given no special authority to make such a claim. Yet a thoughtful answer to the *but why* question will almost always expose secondary or tertiary fronts to attack that are less defensible than the opposition's first-line response. The *but why* challenge should be utilized heavily in the cross-examination periods. Many debaters posit arguments, briefs, and terminology that they simply do not understand. Their opponents can expose this ignorance by using the *but why* technique.

Also, debaters should not simply accept claims of proof that rely upon such mystical sounding phrases as *empirical instantiation* or *correlationally established*. Those phrases merely translate to "it happened once" or "it happened more than once." Debaters should demand the reason why it happened, or inquire as to its cause and effect. After all, correlation does not prove causation. *But why, but why, but why* is no less effective now than it was in kindergarten.

2. The "huh-uh" denial

Imagine you are near a kindergarten play area, where two five-year-old scholars have engaged in a debate to extol the virtues of their favorite tricycles. The first explains that hers is made of a light yet durable alloy, has ten all-terrain speeds, and sports an aerodynamic design that will ensure greater velocity and performance. Her companion carefully considers all these reasons and then proudly says, "Mine is blue." Not much of a debate, is it? While the color blue may be a compelling argument, it would be good for the second child to first refute the reasons offered by the other side before adding reasons to support her side.

Good debate is a focused clash over opposing views relating to the topic. Like the owner of the blue tricycle, though, negative debaters all too often totally ignore an affirmative case's specific arguments and resort to reading a prepared case or generic position, however unrelated.

This tactic of avoiding case arguments to instead focus solely on a negative's pet positions injures debate by avoiding clash on substantive issues. It also causes much wasted flow paper, hence needlessly harvested trees, undoubtedly leading to an ecological disaster of biblical proportions. . . . (Oops, sorry. Force of habit. This slippery slope logical fallacy is brought to you by the letter "S.") Back to my point: An unresponded-to argument is a conceded argument. By refusing to answer specific affirmative arguments, the negative grants its opposition a win. The durable alloy, ten all-terrain speeds, and aerodynamic design stand unrefuted by claims of "blueness."

Good debaters don't avoid a focused clash; rather, they create one by engaging in point-by-point refutation. Instead of diverting attention to an unrelated point, they say, "Huh-uh . . . mine is more durable; huh-uh . . . mine has more speeds; huh-uh . . . mine is a better design and can go even faster than yours."

Fulfilling the important and imposing-sounding burden of refutation (or burden of rejoinder) is not too far removed from children responding *huh-uh* when they hear something objectionable. Your debaters should be strongly encouraged to pursue this *huh-uh* line of reasoning, thereby developing good point-by-point refutation skills.

Consider, though, that if a debater merely says *huh-uh* to each point made by her opponent, she will be guilty of making a *statement* rather than an *argument*. As Stephen Toulmin explains in his book *The Uses of Argument*, all arguments should at least have a clear claim (thesis) supported by logical warrants (reasons) founded upon good data (evidence). Unlike their kindergarten counterparts, in other words, debaters who use a *huh-uh* denial must be careful to include substantive reasons for making each claim and offer sufficient evidence to back up their arguments.

At times, reasoning alone is sufficient data to support a point of refutation. For example, if confronting an affirmative that supports a claim with opinion polls or trend data, a negative may use reasoning alone to argue that the affirmative is constructing an *ad populum* fallacy—that is, that merely proving others behave or believe a certain way does not mean that it is the right way to behave or believe. Here, the debater may have to parrot the ageless question asked by parents, "And if everyone else wanted to jump off a cliff, would that make it right?"

In addition to substantiating a *huh-uh* denial, debaters refuting arguments point-by-point should be careful not to fall into the endless *is not/is too* loop, also learned in kindergarten. In rebuttals, arguments should be extended, cogently answering the *but why* question, not just mindlessly repeating earlier claims regardless of subsequent challenges or counterclaims.

3. The "so what" challenge

What a simple yet amazingly powerful weapon of persuasion we have in just saying, "So what?" If someone accuses a kindergartner of wearing glasses or having freckles, the child can either try to deny it (difficult if true), become devastated by peer-induced shame, or dodge the blow by simply responding, "So what?" Even children seem to know that the *so what* challenge takes the wind out of the sails of their tormentors.

This question-response willingly admits—or at worst, refuses to address—the argument the opposition has presented and is prepared to fortify. Instead, it confidently proclaims, "Even if what you say is true, it really does not matter."

Seasoned debaters apply the *so what* test by asking, "*So what* is the impact on my position if this argument is true?" Debaters often call this consideration an *impact challenge*. Every argument that debaters issue should have a direct impact on the resolution. If it does not, the arguer is wasting time. (Be forewarned, though, that wasting time can be an intentional strategic device, designed to trick one's opponent into investing scarce time resources into arguing a position of relatively little merit. This strategy is called a *time suck*, in the ever so linguistically attractive jargon wars.)

Debaters must always, always, always explain the impact of their arguments and/or explain the lack of impact in their opponent's arguments. If an issue has no impact on either the resolution or the criteria in the round, debaters should consider sidestepping that issue by applying the *so what* challenge, even if they have evidence to read or arguments to lodge.

Two other ways of saying *so what* can be found in the jurisdictional issues of topicality and hasty generalization. Such challenges have been called many things through the years, such as *nontopical, extratopical, subtopical, hasty generalization, jurisdiction, justification*, or even the letter abbreviations *hasty G, T*, and *J*. All of these challenges come under the heading of *so what* since they claim that the case, or arguments issued by the affirmative, do not significantly pertain to the resolution, or do not pertain to it at all. Remember that the resolution is supposed to limit the ground of debatable issues. If the affirmative makes arguments that have nothing to do with the topic of the debate, such arguments clearly have no impact upon the debate.

For example, assume the resolution claims that *blue is the best color*, and the affirmative argues that *oranges taste great.* All the negative must do is wrap a *so what* argument in the jargon of topicality and answer the anticipated *but why* question by providing both standards for topicality and specific violations where the affirmative failed to uphold those standards. The negative should toss in some impact arguments, and the round will probably be won.

Or, assume the resolution states that *homelessness is a major problem for the United States of America,* and the affirmative tells about one homeless person as an example and fails to cite further examples. The negative should now label its *so what* argument as a fallacy of hasty generalization, specifically explain why, and describe the deleterious impact of basing a resolutional decision on such a narrow inductive example.

Another area in which debaters should use this technique pertains to the increasingly prevalent *critiques* argued in NCFCA. With a critique, the negative is often asking judges to disregard (or say *so what* to) the impact of affirmative arguments in light of a presumably bigger problem explained in the critique. Likewise, an affirmative must ask, "*So what* is the unique harmful impact to voting affirmative even if the critique's presupposition is true?" Debaters should apply the *so what* test whenever they can.

4. The "that's stupid" retort

Kids can lack subtlety and diplomacy. If they do not like the way something looks, tastes, or smells, they come right out and say it. So should debaters. For example, many affirmatives argue that the enforcement of a resolutional parameter for debate inhibits their creativity. Shouldn't negatives just give a *that's stupid* response? After all, without a fairly defined topic, debaters will never have a clash-oriented discussion or arrive at an informed decision.

All too often, though, debaters allow stupid arguments to stand unchallenged. Some debaters wrongly assume the judge automatically recognizes a stupid argument. Or, a debater might be too embarrassed to come right out and call an argument stupid. (Of course, social niceties correctly restrain us from actually employing the phrase *that's stupid.* This article is definitely not advocating the use of such rude language.) However, debaters should be unafraid to clearly and politely confront stupid arguments. A rhetorically more sensitive way to say the same thing is to claim that an argument is *counterintuitive.* But the debater must then explain why it does not make sense. A claim without a warrant and evidence does not an argument make.

One vast category of arguments that can be refuted with the *that's stupid* retort is found in the rich field of logical fallacies. Debaters explain why an argument is stupid by exposing it as unsupported, inconsistent, contradictory, begging the question, etc.

For the negative to show that the logical outcomes of the affirmative position are foolhardy or absurd is another method of arguing *that's stupid*. Negatives try to expose all of the potential disadvantages and value objections that will accrue if the judge adopts the affirmative's case. In value debates, negatives may also want to extrapolate likely policy implications from the affirmative's value or fact claims.

Another important dimension of reasoning is the *your old man/old lady is a loser* subset of the *that's stupid* category. In the debate round, these arguments are called by the slightly more acceptable rubric of *source indicts*. The debater reads direct attacks against an opponent's source, exposing the author as unqualified, biased, or in some way unfit to be relied upon in the current discussion. As the source loses its credibility, so does the argument.

A variation of *that's stupid* is the phrase *you're stupid*, also used on playgrounds, but highly discouraged in the debate round. To say *you're stupid* is to launch an *ad hominem* attack, which is itself a logical fallacy. Instead of rejecting the *proponent* of a view, debaters should politely reject *the view itself* and explain why it is argumentatively deficient.

5. The "hey, that's mine" claim

It's a familiar scene: A kindergartener sets her favorite crayon down for a second, only to have a classmate swipe it. As soon as she recognizes her loss, she explodes into an apoplectic frenzy, screaming, "Hey, that's mine! Give it back!"

Debaters are much the same, always claiming others' arguments for their own. This tendency to claim others' arguments has been promoted to almost godlike status in the hierarchy of scholastic debate arguments. The jargonists have bestowed the sacred title of *turn around, turn*, or *flip* to these highly revered arguments.

The turn draws largely from the martial arts premise of turning an attacker's mass and/or momentum back against him. In debate, this position claims that the opponents' argument actually works against the opposition instead of in its favor. For example, advocates for a handgun ban may argue that domestic dispute–related handgun injuries are far too high in the status quo but will undoubtedly decrease following a handgun ban, since guns are the weapons of choice in many such disputes. If the opposition can show a propensity in spatting spouses to switch to potentially more deadly alternatives—say hand grenades—they can turn the gun availability argument around *against* the ban proponents by arguing that the very ban that is being proposed would be counterproductive, because even a poorly aimed hand grenade can be more lethal than a well aimed handgun.

It of course gets to be a bit ridiculous when debaters continue swiping each other's arguments, labeling every other one as a turn, or even more annoyingly, as a double turn. Simple refutation is, after all, a *huh-uh* argument, not a *hey, that's mine* argument.

As a final illustration of the correctly employed turn around, some of you may recall the more rhetorically gifted kindergarten scholars who effectively dispensed with their classmates' taunts by invoking this sacred phrase: *Rubber and glue. Rubber and glue. Bounces off me and sticks to you.* That's what a debater would want to do with his opponent's arguments: explain how the argument does not "stick" to his own position but instead bounces back to "stick" against his opponent's position. In the process, it is not recommended that debaters employ this specific verbiage past the third grade.

Conclusion

The novice debater should not become too discouraged trying to comprehend the recent state of debate terminology. That comprehension will come quickly enough. Instead, she should rely on reasoning skills—which for most of us were adequately honed in kindergarten—to cope with many entry-level debate issues.

By the way, I am still a little unclear on categorizing some of the other cryptic terms I'm hearing in debate rounds these days. Next time you see a group of five-year-olds, will you ask them, for me, to explain what a *permutation* is? I suspect it may belong in the *hey, that's mine* category.

References

Fulghum, Robert. *All I Really Need to Know I Learned in Kindergarten: Uncommon Thoughts on Common Things.* New York: Villard Books, 1988.

Goodnight, T. G. "The Personal, Technical, and Public Spheres of Argument: A Speculative Inquiry into the Art of Public Deliberation." *The Journal of the American Forensic Association,* 18 (1982): 214–227.

Lake, R. A., and B. Haynie. "Post-modernism, Academic Debate and the Public Sphere." In *Argument and the Postmodern Challenge: Proceedings of the Eighth SCA/AFA Conference on Argumentation,* edited by R. E. McKerrow, 17–23. Annandale, VA: Speech Communication Association, 1993

Meyer, J. "The Collaborative Development of Power in Children's Arguments." *Argumentation and Advocacy,* 29 (1992), 77–88.

O'Keefe, B. J., and P. J. Benoit. "Children's Arguments." In *Advances in Argumentation*, edited by J. R. Cox and C. A. Willard, 154–83. Carbondale, IL: Southern Illinois University Press, 1982.

Reike, R. D., and M. L. Willbrand. "Reason Giving in Children's Supplicatory Compliance Gaining." *Communication Monographs*, 53 (1986): 47–60.

Skip Rutledge, Ph.D. candidate, serves on the NCFCA Board of Directors and is Director of Forensics at Point Loma Nazarene University, where he has taught speech, debate, and rhetoric since 1989.

CHAPTER OUTLINES

Rhetorical Influences on Academic Debate

Free people living in a free society have a responsibility to participate in important societal decisions. A free society emphasizes the importance of sharing ideas and coming to agreement about what is the best course of action for the society to take. An essential foundation for the person seeking agreement from an audience is *rhetoric*—that is, communication that attempts to affect the beliefs, attitudes, and actions of others. A common method for this communication is public debate. While rhetoric includes other forms of public speaking in addition to debate, debate is certainly an important type of rhetoric.

Scholars have identified several stages of rhetorical history, each making a unique contribution to the practice of debate. The ancient period contributed a worldview that embedded public speaking into the workings of a society. The British period contributed codification of rhetoric into systems and categories, many of which we still use today. These are the two Golden Ages of Rhetoric identified by rhetorical scholars, and some claim that the present time constitutes a third golden age. The Contemporary Period emphasizes language as an essential element of meaning and of understanding reality.

Understanding how rhetorical theory has birthed debate theory deepens a debater's sense of how the skills learned in this text will contribute to her overall speaking skills. Of course, those skills have power far beyond the debate round, providing the debater-citizen with the tools for presenting all sorts of proposals for change and with the means for discussing value decisions in society.

I. ANCIENT ATHENIAN PERIOD: INCORPORATION OF A WORLDVIEW

The first Golden Age of Rhetoric focused on the relationship between public speaking and important aspects of public life. Athenian democracy operated with freemen meeting to discuss and decide matters of importance to the general public in order to discover political truth. Each man was responsible to speak for himself in the polis (public square). It thus became important for young boys to be trained in rhetoric in order to learn how best to defend their ideas in the public court.

This age of rhetoric also contributed to our modern understanding of communicating from a worldview perspective. For the ancients, the relationship between speaking and public life permeated their view of education for the young speaker.

TEACHER'S NOTES:

▷ Rather than a few experts pleading individuals' cases for hire, each Athenian man was required to plead his own case. Expertise in speaking was necessary in order to be successful in the courts. Aristotle said that if it is a shame that man cannot defend himself from physical attack, how much more a shame that he cannot defend himself with words, when language is that which distinguishes man from the rest of the animal kingdom.

▷ A worldview is a context for understanding and evaluating ideas. New ideas are always considered within the standards of worldview. Our philosophy, or worldview, causes us to see the world in a way that prevents us from seeing other perspectives.

A. Early views of rhetoric

Three early views of rhetorical training addressed the concept of probability, which became a focus of those seeking political truth. Each view held a different perspective of probability and truth.

1. The sophists—The sophists taught that the truth of any issue depended on what the public would accept as true. Corax and Tisias (fifth century, BC) were famous in their time. Corax is credited with developing our courtroom doctrine of probability. Protagoras of Abdera (480–419 BC) is considered the father of debate.

TEACHER'S NOTES:

▷ The sophists did not value truth as an end goal. Sophists placed emphasis on building winning arguments rather than arguments that would point toward the most true position.

▷ Some people wonder about the advisability of students debating both sides of an issue. However, debating both sides of an issue does not make debaters modern-day sophists. Debaters are engaged in an educational activity that employs a specific model of decision making. Learning to debate both sides of a position prepares debaters to be able to argue various issues as they enter the professional world. Seeing an issue from more than one perspective increases understanding of that issue.

2. The idealists: Plato—Plato was the most idealistic of teachers in this camp. He argued that a rhetorician must know his subject completely and know his audience well enough to address their "souls." Other teachers of rhetoric espoused a philosophy that was based on a more realistic view of experience and events.

3. The realists: Aristotle—Aristotle is the best-known teacher of rhetoric from the Athenian period. He saw rhetoric as achieving more practical ends than idealistic ends. His position was also more moderate concerning probability than that of the sophists. Aristotle recognized that sometimes one must argue probabilities. The difference between him and the sophists was that he believed that arguing probabilities could eventually lead to truth.

> **a) Theory of rhetoric**—Aristotle recognized that much of life cannot be proven beyond a doubt; thus, the speaker must depend upon proving what is "probably" the case. Reasoning about probabilities requires more participation from the audience because they must cooperate with the speaker as he builds a likely scenario of what happened. In order to prove what is "probably" the case, the speaker depends upon the authority of the experts.

EXERCISE:

Lead your students in a discussion of several current political issues that cannot be easily proven as "the truth" by either side of the controversy. For example, all acknowledge that the federal government has a constitutional responsibility to provide for the common defense, but the political debate rages over the question of how to accomplish this provision. Will a missile defense system guarantee peace for the United States in coming generations, or will it antagonize nations to act aggressively toward the U.S. in order to prevent the implementation of such a system? We don't know the certain answer to this question, but we can think about what is most likely to happen. This question is therefore a good example of the probability involved in a discussion of political truths.

TEACHER'S NOTE:

Aristotle's definition of rhetoric (discovering all the available means of persuasion) recognizes the probability involved in rhetoric. After discovering all the available means of persuasion, the rhetorician chooses the means most likely to successfully convince the polis of his position, within the bounds of his personal ethical values. The wise Christian seeks to choose only those methods of persuasion that are ethical in the eyes of God. Also, the

Christian must differentiate between those things that are certain and unchanging and those things that are open to interpretation and persuasion.

---

b) Artistic proof—Aristotle developed methods of proof, or methods to convincingly present one's ideas to the public. The methods to consider here are examples of artistic proof: logos, ethos, and pathos. All three are necessary for proving an argument.

(1) **Logos**—These are "rational justifications" given to the audience to help them believe what is said.

TEACHER'S NOTE:

See pages 51–53 of the textbook for further information on several ways of providing justification for an argument or statement. Certain statements may require only "preexistent knowledge" as a justification. Preexistent knowledge, or common knowledge, could be presented in the form of examples or logical steps taken toward a conclusion. Debaters, however, most often use authoritative evidence in developing their reasons for a decision.

(2) **Ethos**—Listeners demand that those they choose to believe be "worthy of confidence" on the subject and in the particular situation.

(3) **Pathos**—People require that there be a connection between what they are asked to do and their own personal interests. Pathos is traditionally thought of as making an emotional appeal that stirs the audience to connect emotionally with the speaker's call for action.

EXERCISE:

Assign your students to take careful notes during the sermons at their churches and identify the preacher's use of logos, ethos, and pathos throughout the speech. Or, you can use a recorded sermon in class and highlight the appropriate use of the three elements of Aristotle's artistic proof. Remind your students that pathos is used appropriately when the speaker ties the truth of his statements or arguments to the personal interests of his audience. In other words, pathos helps explain to the audience why they should care about the truth or evidence being presented.

TEACHER'S NOTE:

An inappropriate emotional appeal is a manipulation of audience emotion without regard for the reasoning behind the argument being made. A speaker can mislead a susceptible audience by tying the emotion of the appeal to the conclusion of the original argument rather than tying it to the reasoning (or proof) of that argument. Emotion not linked to the reasoning of an argument easily becomes a tool of manipulation. Many people in our society today are seduced by such arguments, even to the point where good, logical counterarguments are often not enough to overcome attractive emotional appeals.

Even though emotional appeals can be difficult to overcome, they must always be addressed. Encourage your debaters to respond to emotional appeals by using strong, substantive arguments that will also resonate emotionally with the judge. As Aristotle taught, pathos should be secondary to logos in an argument, but cannot be ignored— even when responding to an inappropriate emotional appeal made by an opponent. These are some principles that you can teach your debaters to follow as they formulate a response to an emotional argument:

▷ When responding to an opponent's argument, consider the consequences of accepting the conclusion of the argument. If the audience accepts this argument, what have they accepted? You can show the unwanted effects of a decision that is made without regard to its logical consequences.

▷ Another way to defeat this type of argument is first to address and defeat the emotional aspect of the argument, and then apply reason, or logic, to the substantive issue. The combination of these two responses can defeat the emotional argument, but it takes the combination—neither will accomplish it alone.

▷ Remember also that an effective response is composed of both good reasons and persuasive speech. Part of persuasion is presenting your argument in a passionate, interesting, and organized manner that is easy for the average person to understand and appreciate.

B. Athenian forms of inquiry

Athenian thinkers developed forms of inquiry in order to most effectively find the truth.

1. Analytic—This systematic form of inquiry evaluates the validity—but not necessarily the truth—of an argument. The scientific method is an example of analytic inquiry.

2. Dialectic—This system of questions and answers is based upon principles generally held to be true. Dialectic is not a very effective method of inquiry in contemporary times because of the current social emphasis on pluralism. As there are fewer and fewer ideas that the majority of Americans hold as true, it is difficult for a speaker to use a question-and-answer format in order to gain agreement.

3. Rhetoric. This third system of inquiry takes pieces of evidence and then expresses the evidence as arguments presented to the audience for a final decision or judgment. The rhetorical method has become a favored way to come to decisions in modern society since it allows the speaker to address changing social norms. The rhetorical method uses arguments built upon probability, which allows it to adjust to these changes in society and to address questions such as "What is best for our society at this point?"

II. BRITISH PERIOD: CODIFICATION OF RHETORICAL PRINCIPLES

This period is known for taking the ancient classical tradition and codifying it according to rules and systems. Rhetoricians emphasized delivery, style, and the psychology of persuasion through the emotions. Scholars during this time understood the power of persuasion and wanted to apply it to democratic and Christian societies.

Thinkers during this period believed in the average citizen's ability to make a responsible choice when two reasoned positions were presented. Common sense was considered a science that could be coded, studied, and understood by all and was therefore the final judge of arguments of a subjective nature.

TEACHER'S NOTES:

▷ This portion of the text is a good place to discuss with your students the important role that lay judges play in NCFCA debate. It is not necessary to have a seasoned debater or a debate coach judging a round of debate in order for a serious discussion of the resolution to be proficiently decided. The "common person" can make a capable decision if the debaters have done their jobs. Each debater in the round must assume his or her responsibility to make clear, well-explained arguments that are supported by quality evidence.

▷ Richard Whately made the greatest contribution to argumentation theory. (*Argumentation* is the term typically applied to the theory that discusses how to best argue an idea. Debate is the specific application of argumentation theory.) Prima facie, presumption, and burden of proof are concepts introduced by Whately. These concepts form the foundation of stock issues. It is important to note how the concepts that Whately developed also help us understand mankind's condition before God. See "A Christian Response to the British Period" on page 25 of the textbook.

III. CONTEMPORARY PERIOD: EMPHASIS ON LANGUAGE

The contemporary period places an emphasis on language's important role in understanding reality, echoing the classical emphasis on *relativism*. This period also emphasizes *invention*, that is, connecting with an audience through a carefully constructed message.

A. Relativism

The relativistic position holds that nothing is certain or permanent. If the anchor of a common source of meaning is removed from a society, then language can be used as a tool of relativism to mean whatever each user desires it to mean. Language thus assumes a place of primary importance in society since it is used to determine reality. This view of language is often called *the social construction of reality.*

Multiculturalists argue that those who control language control power. By changing the language used, argue multiculturalists, reality will be changed. Someone who believes that we create reality exclusively by our words is relying on an overemphasis on relativism (no certainty) and might engage in using language to advance his agenda as the only acceptable alternative.

B. Invention

Contemporary rhetoric places an emphasis on invention, or the challenge of the discovery of ideas. It involves the process of discovering and adapting ideas that are useful in persuasion. When inventing a message, the speaker must include matters of logos, pathos, and ethos.

Invention connects the speaker's interpretations of the situation to the audience's expectations of the subject. Rhetoric is capable of ranging over the topics, themes, and proofs of previous discourse, and in the process it creates a type of practical wisdom that can be applied in the new situation.

TEACHER'S NOTES:

▷ Because of the contemporary emphasis on language to establish reality and to connect with an audience, the role of debate has again become very important in our society. Christians should view the contemporary emphasis on language as a tool to construct social reality as a double-edged sword. God places a great emphasis on language, which is a tool that can be used for good or evil.

▷ It is impossible to avoid relying on others for much of what we know. In deciding whether to accept what we hear from others, we must apply a standard to evaluate whether to believe what we hear. For the believer, the standard is Scripture. Others might not accept Scripture as their standard; thus, the believer moves from the dialectic to the rhetorical method in order to engage the minds and hearts of those who disagree with him.

▷ God created language, and he controls language, so language is not totally relative. Language is at the heart of the matter for Christians, central to our biblical worldview. Because language has been at the center of God's relationship with man, the Christian cannot ignore her responsibility to communicate clearly and persuasively.

2 Critical Thinking

Critical thinking is understood by argumentation scholars not as a specific outcome but rather as a process that continues throughout one's life. The outcomes or conclusions people reach in most decisions are flexible and can be adjusted in significant or minor ways as one continues to think about a matter. Critical thinking is a never-stagnant, constructive process that is always working toward unveiling truth.

TEACHER'S NOTE:

The adjustments that we make as we work through difficult questions sometimes result in a deeper understanding of what we have always believed or known. In spiritual matters, God often leads his children to truth by leading them in their thinking process. He makes it clear that he wants us to think, to think well, and to think his thoughts after him.

I. THE IMPORTANCE OF CRITICAL THINKING

Every human being must choose whether to follow God. In order to make our thinking conform to the mind of God, we must understand what and how we are thinking. But we often neglect to think about what God would want us to do, or we latch onto beliefs without critically examining them.

DISCUSSION QUESTION:

What are the dangers that accompany a lack of critical thinking? *(We make decisions impulsively; we do not think about the consequences of our behavior; and we do not necessarily conform our thinking or behavior to the will of God.)*

II. THE BENEFITS OF CRITICAL THINKING

A. Understanding your own decisions

The critical thinking process is a great aid to the Christian because it allows us to consider the consequences of our actions and what God would want us to do before making a decision.

B. Making your decisions wisely

Critical thinking protects us from making unwise decisions and also protects us from falling prey to the unfair or dishonest practices of others.

C. Defending your decisions

We must be able to produce good reasons for the decisions we make. Defending our decisions requires us to have knowledge of the area we are thinking about, awareness of our personal priorities, and the ability to show the connection between the two.

III. THE DEFINITION OF CRITICAL THINKING

A. Martin Heidegger

Heidegger taught that thoughts are necessary but not sufficient to thinking. We have many thoughts that do not progress to thinking. Thinking begins when we interact with our thoughts. For Heidegger, the goal of thinking is to disclose what is concealed. Thus, critical thinking can be explained as interacting with thoughts in order to unveil truth.

TEACHER'S NOTES:

▷ Another way to explain Heidegger's concept of critical thinking is to say that when we become conscious of our thoughts and begin to think about thinking, we are engaged in critical thinking.
▷ Heidegger's view of the goal of critical thinking is consistent with biblical truth. Our knowledge is darkened by sin, and we spend life attempting to unveil truth through critical thinking (and through other methods) as directed by the Holy Spirit.

B. Joanne Kurfiss

Value theorist Joanne Kurfiss offers a practical definition of critical thinking. According to Kurfiss, critical thinking is (a) an investigation, (b) that explores issues, and (c) arrives at a conclusion. She divides the process of critical thinking into three corresponding phases: analysis, reflection, and construction.

1. Analysis—This first phase requires logic in order to evaluate arguments made up of at least two statements. The thinker must analyze the argument being made, the topic being discussed, and the speaker's counterargument. Logic evaluates the correctness of a statement.

2. Reflection—When engaging in reflection, the thinker must consider all sides of an issue to understand the strengths and weaknesses of each position.

3. Construction—Critical thinking does not end with simply analyzing and reflecting upon an issue; rather, this form of thinking requires the thinker to take the final step of constructing a conclusion that can be advocated and defended.

TEACHER'S NOTES:

▷ Critical thinking requires analysis, reflection, and construction, but these requirements must always be girded with honesty, genuineness, and love. If the goal is to unveil truth, we must approach critical thinking with a humble and contrite heart. The goal cannot be to win the discussion but rather to seek God with our heart, mind, soul, and strength.

▷ The language and thought of a particular society serve as reflections of that society. Our mass language—our clichés, sound bites, and slogans—has an overwhelming influence on what we think about political candidates, what we purchase at the grocery store, and how we view the rest of the world. Mass language often has a particular agenda—"vote for me," "buy the brand name and not the generic," or "this product will make your life much better." The truth-value of these claims is questionable at best because there is an ulterior motive at the heart of each. Unfortunately, people mistake sound bites, clichés, and slogans in everyday life for valuable arguments. When a new film is being released to VHS or DVD, for example, the advertisement usually ends with mass language such as "make your movie collection complete" or "everyone is buying this movie—own it today," rather than with an appeal to sound logic.

Mass language attempts to make people believe something without giving them good reasons to do so. The average person does not force himself to evaluate whether he logically needs a product or not. Because people often do not think before they act, the line begins to blur between valuable and meaningless mass language. However, the critical thinker works through the claims made in mass language to differentiate between valuable and meaningless mass language.[1]

EXERCISE:

Bring magazine or newspaper advertisements into class and have students critically think about the message contained in the ads. Or, assign students to locate their own ads at home and write a critical analysis of the ads that they find. Have them identify valuable (logical, pertinent) mass language as well as meaningless (emotional, illogical, impulsive) mass language.

IV. THE COMPONENTS OF CRITICAL THINKING

The components of critical thinking are based upon the work of Stephen Brookfield, who identified four practical ways of approaching the process of critical thinking.

A. Identifying and challenging assumptions

In order to understand an argument, debaters must first be able to identify both the argument itself and the assumptions that may underlie the argument. Only then will they be able to properly counter the entirety of an opponent's argument or properly understand the implications of their own arguments and beliefs.

TEACHER'S NOTE:

G. K. Chesterton once said that people quarrel because they do not know how to argue. In other words, true argument requires that people critically examine their own beliefs to look for hidden assumptions, that they test those assumptions against biblical truth, and that they recognize and challenge the assumptions of others—and few seem to possess those prerequisite skills. As a result, people quarrel because they do not know what the other party is really saying, resulting in misunderstandings rather than a discussion of the true issues. While not all quarrels are based upon misunderstandings, clarification of assumptions allows us to begin discussing the real issues at hand.

DISCUSSION QUESTIONS:

▷ What are assumptions? (*Assumptions are reasons that help justify an argument but are not explicitly identified as part of the argument.*)

▷ What are the dangers of failing to identify assumptions as part of decision making or argumentation? (*We can fail to make proper, godly decisions; we can wrongly judge others by stereotyping them.*)

▷ How can you work to identify assumptions before you make decisions? (*Allow students to come up with their own ideas.*)

EXERCISE:

Discuss with your students the fallout from acting upon decisions that are based upon hidden assumptions. Begin with simple instances: John Doe assumes his children know he loves them because he gets up and goes to work each morning to provide for them. Should John challenge this assumption? Progress to instances that are more complex—issues dealing with human nature, perhaps. We assume that all mothers love their children and put their best interests first. This assumption influences child custody laws, advertisements, the celebration of Mother's Day, etc. What other assumptions can you and your students identify in U.S. society?

B. Challenging the importance of context

Context is the environment in which an idea or argument exists. Without understanding the context of an argument, the debater will not be able to adequately argue for or against a particular position because he will not understand the significance of the ideas involved. Context also helps the debater understand how a specific argument or evidence can be applied to the resolution.

C. Imagining and exploring alternatives

This process can be both productive and creative, taking you toward an improved or corrected answer to a situation. Critical thinking is different from a critical spirit—it is not a habit of finding fault with others. It goes beyond destructive responses to both an understanding and examination of why an idea might be wrong and how the problem or issue can be fixed or better understood.

TEACHER'S NOTE:

A student can best learn to imagine how the world could look and function a little differently by reading about an issue from writers who represent a variety of positions on the subject. Sometimes it is the combination of ideas from various sources or various viewpoints that allows the student to find a creative solution to the problem being studied.

EXERCISE:

Plan a class discussion of how the current policy debate topic requires debaters to imagine and explore alternatives. This discussion will lead students to consider how the stock issues provide the elements of the argument that will enable them to convince others that their ideas are good.

D. Engaging in reflective skepticism

The alternatives produced by the affirmative team must satisfy the persuasive requirements of the audience. Engaging in reflective skepticism will therefore help the debater identify weak areas of her argument and either improve or compensate for those areas.

TEACHER'S NOTE:

An important aspect of the Aristotelian view of argumentation includes a willingness to admit that one is wrong. In the round of debate, the debater must advocate his position with confidence. There should, however, be a spot in every debater's thinking where he realizes he could be wrong—that outside the debate round another position might be superior. This realization translates into a humble spirit when working with a partner, other members of the club, or the coach.

Part of your job as the coach is to help students develop this spirit of humility. Although it is human nature to be enamored with our own ideas and to resist the necessary critiques that others can offer, it is important for students to learn how to receive criticism from the teacher or coach. It is easy for beginning debaters, especially, to believe that all of their ideas are innately good and should be adopted by others. This illusion must be dispelled. It is not often the case that anyone presents an idea that is perfectly formed and satisfactorily supported on the first writing. It is important for the student to "play the devil's advocate" and challenge her own case before holding it up to the scrutiny of others.

As you help students prepare their arguments and cases, your job will be to assist students' efforts to think critically about their own arguments and identify the best possible arguments to run in the round. The advice you give to your students should be accepted readily, and they should be willing to change their arguments or cases accordingly.

DISCUSSION QUESTION:

▷ In what specific ways can you apply the principle of reflective skepticism to academic debate? (*Reflective skepticism will cause the debater to take special care to develop all of the stock issues and double-check the appropriate links within the case; reflective skepticism can also be applied to the analysis of evidence, both the debater's own evidence and that of his opponent.*)
▷ Can you brainstorm even more ways of applying reflective skepticism to the activity of debate?

FOR FURTHER STUDY:

Having *the desire* to think critically or understanding the components of critical thinking is not enough for a debater to succeed in accomplishing this task. He must also *develop the skills* to think critically. A student does not have to be an intellectual genius to possess these skills—they can be learned and developed by the average person. Brooke Moore and Richard Parker present skills which assist in learning how to think critically. These skills include the ability to listen and read carefully, to evaluate arguments, to look for and to find hidden assumptions, and to trace the consequences of a claim.[2]

▷ *Listen and read carefully.* This skill requires attention and mental discipline. When listening to an argument or reading a piece of potential evidence, the critical thinker pays special attention to what is being said, looking for clues as to the strong and weak points of the argument. In far too many debate rounds that I (Deb) have judged, I have heard one team read a piece of evidence that weakens or condemns its position, only to see the opposing team's heads buried in the flow sheet, oblivious to what has actually been said. For example, in the outrounds at the 2002 NCFCA Nationals, a debater read a piece of negative evidence in an attempt to defend the status quo. This evidence claimed that the status quo was "looking at" several options for change, one of which was the change proposed by the affirmative case. If someone on the affirmative team had been listening, he would have been able to turn this evidence to prove that the affirmative plan was sufficiently workable and solvent enough that policy makers were considering it as an option, that it had not yet been implemented within the status quo because of some inherent problem within the status quo, and that only the affirmative plan could bring this excellent option to life as U.S. policy. But because the affirmative wasn't listening, this winning argument was not made, and by the end of the round, the negative team was arguing that the affirmative case was already part of the status quo! An argument that could have clinched an affirmative win had now become a liability.

▷ *Evaluate arguments.* The first step here is to identify the main points of the argument. These main points are the basis for what is being argued and must cohere for the argument to be credible: *Have all the inferences necessary to the argument been stated? Will the parts of the argument allow you to draw a different conclusion if you apply different inferences?*

The second step is to examine the structure of the argument to determine if the parts fit together to make a reasonable whole: *Do the steps of the argument flow together to make the claim you are trying to make? Do the real-world examples that illustrate each point of the argument prove your overall claim? If the argument were accepted and taken to its conclusion, would the consequences be desirable?*

Finally, understand what the entirety of the argument means in relation to the question at hand. If your case is based on the philosophy that a freer trade policy with developing countries will help to promote democracy, you could not argue that open trade with Sudan would reduce human rights abuses and thus improve the chances for democracy while at the same time arguing that trade sanctions against Iraq will cause the people to rise up and overthrow Saddam Hussein, ushering in democracy. Because these two arguments contradict one another, you would need to choose which argument is stronger.

▷ *Examine the underlying assumptions.* Arguments almost always possess underlying assumptions that have been taken for granted and are unstated. It is wise to determine what these assumptions are in order to make the decision whether one will accept or challenge the assumptions in addition to the argument itself. This skill is discussed at length as a component of critical thinking. Moore and Parker agree that examining underlying assumptions is a skill because the ability to evaluate assumptions is learned.

The Romans used the term *caveat emptor* in their business dealings—"to the buyer, beware." If a Roman bought an object without examining the seller's reputation and questioning him about its quality and authenticity, then the buyer deserved an inferior product if that is what he was sold.

Accepting an argument on its face value needs a mental *caveat emptor*. If you fail to examine the quality of the assumptions underlying an argument, you will be vulnerable to accepting inferior arguments.

Challenging assumptions helps us to avoid following a particular practice or behavior out of habit or tradition. When challenged, we are able to consider the habit and ask, "Why do I think or act in this way?" The person engaged in critical thinking takes action based on the answer to that question. He might decide to keep the habit or practice because he can defend it adequately; decide to keep the practice but gain more information about the practice so that he can defend it better; or decide to change, realizing that this practice is self-destructive, is in violation of God's Word, or is based on an emotional foundation.

▷ *Trace the consequences of a claim.* It is natural for a person to take into consideration the consequences of an action before committing that action. Our legal system is partly based upon this principle. The knowledge of what my punishment will be when I break a law keeps me from doing something illegal. Knowledge of consequences can motivate us to welcome or avoid behaviors. What are the consequences of granting amnesty to illegal aliens now residing in the United States? Do we want these consequences to materialize? Looking forward to consequences becomes an important element in critical decision making.

You can use the four skills outlined here to supplement your explanation of critical thinking for your students. In debate, these skills should help your students properly evaluate and critique the resolution as well as each argument they make or face from their opponents. It might seem overwhelming and time-consuming at first, but once your students learn the process, it will become easier and easier for them to automatically apply these four steps of critical thinking to their decision making until the critical thinking process becomes second nature.

Outline 2 Endnotes

[1] Annette T. Rottenberg, *Elements of Argument: A Text and Reader* (New York: St. Martin's Press, 2000), 188.

[2] Brooke N. Moore and Richard Parker, *Critical Thinking*, 3d ed. (Mountain View, CA: Mayfield Publishing Company, 1992), 5.

3 Tests of Evidence

OUTLINE

I. THE HUMAN NEED FOR EVIDENCE

Since we are born with finite knowledge, all humans need evidence in order to form opinions or arrive at conclusions. The Bible itself serves as evidence of God and is the primary way that we learn about God.

EXERCISE:

Have the student look for ways evidence is used every day. Perhaps he could read the newspaper, watch the evening news, or listen to a sermon in order to find uses of evidence.

II. TYPES OF EVIDENCE

A. Physical evidence

This type of evidence consists of those things that we discover by use of our five senses.

B. Testimony

Evidence in the form of testimony consists of the oral or written account of someone who observed evidence firsthand.

C. Opinions

Opinions are conclusions based upon the other kinds of evidence, or interpretations of what the other kinds of evidence really mean. Opinion evidence explains why something is significant or meaningful.

EXERCISES:

Have your students complete the following exercises:

▷ Give three examples of physical evidence that you have seen, felt, tasted, touched, or heard this week.

▷ Give three examples of testimony that you have heard or read in the past.

▷ Give three examples of opinions that you have heard or read about current events.

III. THE HIERARCHY OF EVIDENCE

A hierarchy is simply a method of grading something from best to worst. In a hierarchy of evidence, the best evidence is at the top and the worst is at the bottom. Make sure the student understands the definition of a hierarchy.

EXERCISE:

Have the student categorize the foods that he eats into a hierarchy, from the best food to the worst food. Discuss how the hierarchy should be constructed and what values should be used. Should the student's taste preferences be the determining value? Should health be the determining value? The construction of the hierarchy will depend upon the value being used. This exercise will help lay the foundation for the concepts presented in Chapters 11, 12, and 13 of the textbook regarding value debate.

IV. TESTS OF EVIDENCE

Tests of evidence are tools that we can use to determine the quality of evidence.

A. Test the source.

1. Bias—A bias is an inclination or leaning of the mind in a certain direction.

2. Primary versus secondary sources—Primary sources are sources that have firsthand information. Secondary sources repeat what they know from others.

3. Expertise—Expertise involves education, respect, and knowledge of the subject area.

4. Fact versus opinion—Facts are objective and able to be verified; opinions are subjective and cannot be completely verified.

DISCUSSION QUESTIONS:

▷ Is bias good or bad? *(It is neither good nor bad. Everyone has biases. The important thing is to identify the bias and whether or not the bias negatively affects the accuracy of the evidence.)*

▷ Give some examples of bias that you've come across in the last week.

▷ What is the difference between a primary and a secondary source? *(A primary source has had firsthand observation or experience of the evidence. A secondary source is repeating the evidence that came from someone else.)*

▷ How do you know if someone is an expert? *(An expert is a person who is well-educated and well-respected in the subject area.)*

▷ What is the difference between facts and opinions? *(Facts can be verified by either physical observation or firsthand testimony. Opinions are subjective interpretations of evidence and cannot be physically verified.)*

▷ What kinds of qualities are the best qualities that a source of evidence can have? *(The best sources of evidence are experts in the subject area, free from self-interested bias, who have directly observed or experienced the evidence in question and who base their opinions on those facts.)*

B. Test the date.

DISCUSSION QUESTION:

Is the best evidence always the most recent evidence? *(No, because the date of the evidence does not necessarily affect the true application of the evidence to the question at hand. Older evidence may be used if it still accurately applies to today's situations.)*

C. Test the consistency.

1. Consistency with the tagline—A good piece of evidence will prove exactly what the tagline says it proves.

2. Consistency with the publication as a whole—A good piece of evidence does not contradict the source from which it came.

3. Consistency with other sources of evidence—A good piece of evidence can be supported with evidence from other sources.

D. Test the text.

1. Vague terminology—Vague terminology consists of words that are undefined and too vague to be meaningful. Simply saying something is "bad" doesn't really tell us what is wrong with it.

2. Qualifying language—Qualifying language consists of words that limit the statement being made, such as *probably, may, sometimes,* or *often.*

EXERCISE:

Have the student find examples of vague terminology and qualifying language in a daily newspaper or magazine. Discuss how these examples weaken what is being said and how these weaknesses can be improved. *(Note: Qualifying language is often necessary so that the author does not overstate his case. If the qualifying language is necessary, then it is not a weakness per se, for the truth is never a weakness. But you can find the weak spots in a person's argument by looking for language that qualifies the overall claim.)*

E. Test the statistics.

1. Surveys and polls—These forms of measurement are never 100 percent accurate and always contain a margin of error, as well as other sources of error such as the time of day that the survey was taken, the number of days that it took to conduct the poll, and the way the questions were asked.

2. Percentages—Numbers in the form of percentages can be misleading, especially if the actual numbers are small. It is always helpful to know what the "real" numbers are behind the percentages.

3. Comparison—Numbers need a meaningful context in order to be accurately understood. Comparing numbers with a known standard provides a meaningful context for those numbers. For example, stating that you have a big family because you have 10 children isn't meaningful unless we know that the average family has only 2.5 children.

DISCUSSION QUESTIONS:

▷ Do you think that surveys and polls are accurate enough to be helpful sources of evidence for debate?

▷ If so, how would you make sure that evidence from a survey or poll is as accurate as possible? *(Look for evidence from well-respected sources; look at the hard numbers behind the percentages reported in the poll; and look for a large sample size, i.e., a lot of people were included in the study.)*

▷ How can you make statistical evidence understandable for your audience? *(Keep numbers simple; don't read a lot of numbers at once; use real-life examples that illustrate the numbers; and test statistical evidence by reading it to family and friends before using it in the debate round.)*

▷ How does comparison make statistics meaningful? *(Without a standard of comparison, we don't know if a number is bigger than usual, smaller than usual, or average.)*

4 Using Evidence Persuasively

I. PERSUASIVE TECHNIQUES

These techniques will help the debater orally present her evidence in a way that is easy for the audience to listen to and understand. Have your students practice these techniques when they engage in practice debates.

A. Taglines

A persuasive debater reads an accurate, interesting tagline just before she reads her evidence.

B. Repetition

A good speaker always repeats important points. A good rule is the rule of three: tell your audience what you're going to say, say it, then tell them what you've said.

C. Organization

A persuasive speaker is organized. It is very difficult to understand a disorganized speech.

D. Audience analysis

A good debater speaks to her audience using evidence that they will respect and using arguments that resonate with audience members' particular interests or beliefs.

E. Warrant for attacks

Rather than simply stating that her opponent is wrong, a persuasive debater explains *why* her opponent's evidence or arguments are poor.

EXERCISE:

Have the student listen to a sermon (at church or on tape) and note what persuasive techniques the pastor uses (or does not use). Have the student explain how attention to these techniques made the sermon persuasive or how lack of attention to these techniques made the sermon difficult to understand. *(Note: Some techniques, like taglines, are not directly applicable to sermons. Instead, have the student look for whether or not the pastor summarizes Scripture passages into understandable phrases or points. Likewise, a sermon does not directly attack an opponent's speech, but often the pastor will refute arguments against Christianity or provide a defense against faulty understandings of theology.)*

DISCUSSION QUESTIONS:

▷ What are the qualities of a good tagline? *(Clarity, conciseness, accuracy, confidence, and colorful, interesting language.)*

▷ What are audiences most likely to remember? *(Beginnings and endings.)*

▷ What kind of audience are you most likely to face if you debate in NCFCA? *(Answer from your own personal knowledge.)*

▷ What is a "warrant" for an attack? *(A "warrant" is evidence that proves a claim.)*

▷ Why is it important to have warrants for your attacks? *(Without a warrant, there is no reason for the audience to know why your attack is important. An attack without a warrant is an argument without any reasoning.)*

II. QUALITIES OF PERSUASIVE EVIDENCE

A. Length

A good piece of evidence will generally be two or three sentences long.

B. Simplicity

A good piece of evidence is easy for the average listener to understand.

C. Content

A good piece of evidence will say what you want it to say.

D. Documentation

A good piece of evidence will contain enough information so that listeners can look it up and verify its accuracy.

E. Honesty

A good piece of evidence will be scrupulously gathered so that it is an accurate quote faithful to the letter and intent of the original work. It will also be honest according to the debater's own knowledge of the issue.

TEACHER'S NOTE:

Many in the NCFCA league have been hesitant to provide copies of evidence when asked in the debate round. Sometimes the opposing team will ask to look at a piece of evidence or a copy of the affirmative case. Other times, the judge will wish to examine a particular quotation. In either case, the honest, prepared debater will cheerfully provide the requested evidence with no hesitation.

This practice is not only a matter of common courtesy but also a matter of honesty. Why should the debater not permit his evidence to be examined? Is he afraid his opponents will find that he has been quoting it incorrectly? Is he afraid his opponents will find that he has been claiming more than the evidence actually proves? Is he afraid his opponents will see all the weaknesses of his case? The prepared debater will not be afraid of any of these scenarios because he will have quoted every piece of evidence correctly and constructed a case of which he is proud.

Instruct your students to have copies of the affirmative case on hand to provide to the opposing team and to have copies of key pieces of evidence that the other team or judge may wish to see during the round. The judge may also wish to look at evidence after the round to clarify a point or to examine it for honesty. Your students should always be happy to put their evidence on the line for examination and have nothing to hide.

There are two important caveats to this general principle. First, if your students do not use a written case to give the first affirmative constructive (1AC), then they naturally cannot provide a copy to the opposing team. Instead, you can offer the outline your student used to make his speech as well as any evidence that was quoted in the 1AC. Second, providing the opposing team with a copy of the case is a *common courtesy* and not a league rule. However, the judge may perceive a lack of willingness to share the case as an attempt at dishonesty or rudeness, and teams that do not provide at least an outline of the case and/or evidence when requested can harm their credibility with the judge.

EXERCISE:

Allow your students to practice cutting good pieces of evidence from two or three newspaper or magazine articles that you provide. These articles would ideally cover topics that are relevant to the current resolution you are studying. Have each student work independently, so that several students are separately examining the same article. When they are finished, compare the quotations they have cut and discuss the differences, both positive and negative.

III. SOURCES OF EVIDENCE

There are basically two places to find evidence: on the Internet and in a library. Caution your students about the dangers of Internet sources and make sure they understand what constitutes trustworthy evidence. The following questions and exercises should help.

EXERCISES:

▷ Take your students to the local library or local university to acquaint them with the library system. Ideally, you could set up an appointment with the reference librarian and have him show your group what the library offers and how to use its reference materials.

▷ Find several pieces of evidence on the same subject from a variety of websites, some reputable and some untrustworthy. (The subject doesn't have to be serious—it could be anything from flowers to football.) Then have your students identify the sites that are the most trustworthy and explain why. Discuss the content of the evidence and how it varies from site to site. Or, for an advanced student, have the student do the research himself and identify trustworthy versus untrustworthy sites for one subject.

DISCUSSION QUESTIONS:

▷ Why is material on the Internet not completely trustworthy? *(Anyone can publish online; there are no barriers such as good editors, finances, or an established reputation.)*

▷ What are the best kinds of Internet sites for gathering evidence? *(Sites which publish evidence that is already in the mainstream: government reports, law reviews, court decisions, congressional legislation, etc.; sites that have a good journalistic or academic reputation.)*

5 **Absolute Voting Issues**

Academic debate is rooted in classical rhetorical concepts that create an understood context in which the debate occurs. As with all competitive activities, debate relies upon certain standards that most judges use to make their decisions during a debate round. There are two foundational standards—prima facie and topicality—that must be understood in order for a team to win a hearing from the judge. These standards are related to essential rhetorical concepts.

I. RHETORICAL CONCEPTS OF DEBATE

A. Presumption

Presumption is the name given to the concept that life (or society or government) will continue as we know it until there is sufficient reason to change. Because humans do not easily throw over one way of living for another in either trivial or essential areas of life, presumption assumes that the current system is justified until we are convinced otherwise. It is for this reason that the negative team in the debate round waits for an indictment of the present system before speaking.

TEACHER'S NOTE:

Presumption could be compared with the legal concept that a person is innocent until proven guilty. Thus, in a criminal trial, the prosecution must present the state's case against the defendant before the defendant responds.

EXERCISE:

Have the class think of other areas of life where presumption operates.

B. Burden of proof

Burden of proof is the complement to presumption: if the status quo enjoys presumption, then those who wish to change the status quo must show good and sufficient reason to do so. In academic debate, *the burden of proof* is a special responsibility given to the affirmative team which must be satisfied in the 1AC. The best way to meet the burden of proof is to plan the 1AC according to the stock issues.

A burden of proof (or *burden of rejoinder*) is the responsibility of each debater who advances a claim. This concept can be summarized as "he who asserts must prove." In other words, the negative team also possesses a responsibility to prove its own assertions against the affirmative case.

TEACHER'S NOTES:

▷ The affirmative responsibility to prove its case does not end after the 1AC. After fulfilling *the burden of proof* by presenting a prima facie case in the first speech, the affirmative will continue to have a *burden* to prove its case after each negative attack. If the negative attacks a case point in a subsequent speech, the burden shifts back to the affirmative team to rebuild that part of the case. Affirmatives should also keep in mind that because they possess the overall burden of proof, the judge will often weigh individual stock issue arguments according to principles of burden of proof and presumption. For example, a judge may presume in favor of a negative solvency argument unless the affirmative consistently offers very convincing counterarguments throughout the round.

▷ Because the negative team possesses the burden of rejoinder, the negative must respond to the entire affirmative case in the first negative constructive (1NC). The 1NC should never spend the entire speech just arguing against topicality and prima facie. If the affirmative case stands unrefuted after the 1NC and the judge decides the affirmative case is both topical and meets prima facie requirements, there is nothing for the second negative speaker to argue—she cannot go back to the affirmative case. The burden of rejoinder against the affirmative case *resides in the 1NC* just as the burden of proof for the affirmative resides in the 1AC. (Of course, the burden of rejoinder exists only after the affirmative team has met its burden to present a prima facie case in the 1AC.) Then, as each speaker meets the burden of his or her side of the debate, the burden will continue to shift throughout the round. Just as the affirmative cannot "surprise" the negative by stringing out its burden of proof throughout the round and presenting an incomplete case for change in the 1AC, the negative cannot "surprise" the affirmative and string out its burden of rejoinder by failing to present its response against the entire affirmative case in the 1NC.

This theory of burden of proof and rejoinder is one that keeps the negative from "splitting the negative." When a debate team splits the negative, the first negative speaker addresses only half of the affirmative case and saves the other half for the second negative speaker to address. In other words, the negative ignores parts of the 1AC stock issue arguments and addresses them for the first time in the second negative constructive (2NC).

Saving the negative response to certain stock issues until the 2NC violates principles of fairness. If the affirmative must present a complete case for change in its first speech, then the negative should present a complete case in favor of the status quo in its first speech.

Furthermore, it is the opinion of the editors of this text that the practice of splitting the negative will eventually lead to what is referred to as a "speed and spread" style of debate: When the affirmative team does not know all of the stock issue attacks the negative will make against its case until the 2NC, it is left without the information it needs in order to respond appropriately to the arguments that are central to the round. In order to overcome this natural negative advantage, the affirmative often tries to "spread" its case by making it longer and more involved. A longer case requires a longer response from the negative team, thus neutralizing some of the advantage the negative gained by "splitting." However, in order to read a long case in eight minutes, the affirmative must "speed" through it by speaking much faster than the average listener can understand.

The editors of this text do not believe that the speed and spread style of debate helps meet the goal of training Christian students to speak to a lost world. We are not merely teaching students how to think quickly or maneuver their way through a game; rather, we are teaching students how to persuade the average listener. If students do not practice communicating what are sometimes complicated ideas to an average audience, they will not have learned the important skills required to explain Christian principles to a world that doesn't understand Christ.

II. ABSOLUTE VOTING ISSUES

Absolute voting issues are jurisdictional requirements that must be met by the affirmative team in order for a debate to take place. The judge must decide whether to listen to a debate or an affirmative case based upon whether or not the affirmative case meets the necessary jurisdictional qualifications.

TEACHER'S NOTES:

▷ When a team brings a case to you to evaluate, the first two gates through which it must pass are *topicality* and *prima facie*. The affirmatives must fulfill these burdens. These issues are "absolute" because the affirmative team should automatically lose the round if it fails to carry both issues.

Topicality and prima facie are concerned with procedure because they are absolutely necessary for the debate to be grounded in the resolution. If the affirmative presents a case that does not address the resolution, then there is no purpose to the debate. The debate must be grounded in the resolution so that the negative is able to prepare for the discussion.

Because the resolution is the focus of the debate, the affirmative must talk about the resolution as it is worded—not some variation of the resolution. It is important for affirmatives to understand this responsibility and the need for a carefully crafted case that addresses both absolute voting issues.

▷ Judges vary as to the degree to which they will intervene in these matters. Some judges have difficulty giving the affirmative team a loss for one of these reasons even when the negative team presents a well-developed argument. Other judges will intervene if they determine that a prima facie case has not been presented, acting on their own initiative even if not asked to do so by the negative team. Most judges will not intervene in the matter of topicality, but instead wait for the negative team to make the argument. But remember that every judge is different—as soon as you think you can predict what one is going to do, you will be surprised.

These jurisdictional arguments are complicated matters that at times require intricate arguments. It is the debaters' responsibility to demonstrate to the judge that they understand how these requirements affect a round of debate.

▷ The absolute voting issues require that a debater be able to see how the arguments in an affirmative case work in relation to one another. The ability to see how ideas fit together in an argument is an important critical thinking skill that your debaters are learning when they work through the application of absolute voting issues. The time you spend in class or in club working on these issues will certainly be time well spent.

A. Prima facie

Prima facie is a term used in debate and in American law courts that means "at first glance." The elements of a prima facie case have for years been seen as the issues which must be addressed in order to overcome presumption and to justify changing from the status quo to a new system.

The prima facie case is defined as a case that a reasonable person can consider strong enough to stand unless it is refuted. The first time a judge hears the affirmative reasons for adopting the resolution, the reasons should be complete and developed well enough that the negative must answer in order to win. (The idea that the negative "must answer in order to win" is the "burden of rejoinder.") A prima facie case therefore dislodges presumption and is the first essential step in fulfilling the burden of proof.

The necessary elements of a prima facie case are topicality and presentation of all of the stock issues. All of these elements must be presented in the 1AC speech. When this is accomplished, the affirmative can claim to have met the burden of proof of the 1AC.

B. Topicality

Many debate theorists see topicality as both an absolute voting issue and a stock issue.

1. Definitions—A topical defense begins with definitions, because definitions show the affirmative's interpretation of the resolution. Topicality requires the affirmative to uphold every term in the resolution.

TEACHER'S NOTE:

There is a difference between the negative redefining a term and running a topicality charge. When a negative makes a topicality charge based on a definitional problem, it is charging that a particular definition causes the case to fail to uphold the resolution. When the negative attacks an affirmative definition on grounds *other* than topicality, it is merely arguing about a particular word without making any claims that the definition impacts the topicality of the case. Only a topicality charge is an absolute voting issue; an argument over definitions alone is treated like any other argument. If negatives do not redefine terms or charge a topicality offense, then they must argue within the parameters of the affirmative definitions.

2. Case content—The affirmative team's second responsibility with regard to the issue of topicality is to present a case that fulfills every aspect of the resolution. The affirmative cannot add to the resolution or fail to address any part of the resolution. It is especially important for the affirmative to incorporate the action required by the resolution into the plan or to address the value conflict named in the resolution within the contentions.

When planning a case, the affirmative team should pay attention to the relationships that are drawn between the various parts of the case and the resolution. The affirmative case must uphold its own interpretation of the words in the resolution.

TEACHER'S NOTES:

▷ Negatives must follow proper procedure when running a topicality charge.

▷▷ First, negatives should present the standard that affirmatives must follow in regard to proper definitions (e.g., *"Affirmatives must consider the field context of their definitions. In economics, the term* interest *means one thing but in the field of law, something entirely different"*). For definition standards, see Chapter 9 of the textbook.

▷▷ Second, negatives must show how the affirmative team has violated this standard.

▷▷ Third, negatives must redefine the term in dispute. If the negatives offer no counter-definition, then the affirmative definition, even though flawed, must stand. The word has to mean something.

▷ Teach your students the following affirmative principles for responding to a negative topicality charge:

▷▷ The affirmative team must take every topicality charge very seriously.

▷▷ Affirmatives should begin their defense in the cross-examination of the 1NC. The goal is to weaken the charge as much as possible.

▷▷ The second affirmative speaker addresses topicality in the second affirmative constructive (2AC) and spends the time necessary to explain the case and show it is topical. She should answer the topicality attack *first*—before answering any other negative arguments—by addressing the standards, the violation, and the impact presented by the negative team, in that order.

▷▷ Refutation and rebuttal of the topicality argument continues in each cross-examination and in each speech until the end of the round.

▷▷ If the negative team drops the charge, the affirmative emphasizes to the judge that the charge goes away, and the judge should no longer consider topicality as a voting issue at the end of the round.

▷ Theoretically, the judge decides the two absolute voting issues early in the round. There are two reasons for this. First, remember that the underlying principle for absolute voting issues is that unless these two threshold requirements are met, the judge is not "authorized" to listen to the affirmative arguments. The second reason is related to making a differentiation between absolute voting issues and stock issues, which must also be carried by the affirmative for an affirmative win.

How, then, do the stock issues differ from the absolute voting issues? An absolute voting issue has a more authoritative quality than the other voting issues. In debate, most scholars agree that the authoritative difference is that the absolute voting issues must be answered first, before any other issues can be considered. Stock issues are then argued by each speaker on each side of the resolution for the duration of the debate. At the conclusion of the debate, the judge decides which team made the strongest, most convincing argument on each stock issue. This makes each stock issue a voting issue.

When deciding on the stock issue of solvency, for instance, the affirmative might solve for the harm, but the negative might have presented a serious disadvantage that seems to outweigh the harm. Thus, the judge must weigh the affirmative advantage of solving the harm against the negative disadvantage of creating a new problem in the system.

But when deciding on the absolute voting issues of topicality and prima facie, it is all-or-nothing for the affirmative team. The judge does not weigh what the affirmative says against some different but related negative argument. Instead, the judge considers the violation of topicality or prima facie that the negative claims, listens to the affirmative answer, and decides yes or no—either the affirmative meets or does not meet the requirement. The judge can make this decision anytime in the round that he chooses, but typically the debate will continue to the end of the round, without the participants knowing the judge's decision.

EXERCISE:

Have your debaters practice arguing absolute voting issues in a round. Assign some of your debaters the task of launching each of the absolute voting issue attacks, and others the task of refuting those attacks.

DISCUSSION QUESTION:

How do the absolute voting issues differ from the stock issues? *(Absolute voting issues are procedural issues that the affirmative must meet in order to win the right to present arguments on the stock issues. The stock issues, on the other hand, are substantive issues that help affirmative teams overcome the average person's presumption in favor of the status quo by answering all of the questions most people have before being willing to make a change. The judge can decide an absolute voting issue at any point in the round by measuring the affirmative against definite procedural standards; however, the stock issues are not so absolute and are weighed against all of the argumentation presented throughout the round before the judge votes.)*

6 Stock Issues

Because stock issues provide a format that guarantees the inclusion of the essential elements of a decision-making exercise, they are important in our everyday lives. In both policy and value debate, stock issues share equal importance and perform the same function: to help overcome presumption and fulfill the burden of proof. However, debaters in each form of debate emphasize the stock issues differently.

TEACHER'S NOTES:

▷ Help students to see that stock issues are not mysterious. These are common-sense requirements we place on ourselves and others whenever an important decision must be made.

▷ Stock issues relate to absolute voting issues in a round of debate. In other words, addressing stock issues increases the likelihood of the affirmative meeting all of its burdens.

   ▷▷ A *prima facie case* (which is created by addressing all of the stock issues accurately) is important in the first affirmative speech because it dislodges *presumption*.

   ▷▷ A *prima facie case* fulfills the 1AC's responsibility to satisfy *the burden of proof*.

   ▷▷ By presenting all the stock issues in the 1AC, the affirmative reduces the possibility of a *topicality* charge from the negative team.

▷ It is wise to teach these concepts early and to repeat them each time your club meets or each time you are teaching this subject. The concepts seem overwhelming to debaters at first, but they become familiar friends with repetition. Also, it is best to teach these ideas in relationship to one another because, in the long run, the connection of concepts will help simplify the matter for students.

EXERCISE:

Choose two or three examples of decisions people make in the course of their lives. Evaluate each sample decision by applying the questions listed on page 99 of the textbook:

▷ *Why is this important?*

▷ *Why hasn't the problem been fixed before?*

▷ *So what if this problem exists?*

▷ *What can we do about this problem?*

▷ Will this correction make a difference?
▷ What are the drawbacks?
▷ Will the situation be worse when we are done?

I. STOCK ISSUES FOR POLICY DEBATE

The stock issues work together to create a complete case for change. The most common stock issues discussed in debate texts are topicality, significance, inherence, and solvency.

A. Understanding specific stock issues

1. Topicality—Topicality is an absolute voting issue that is also considered an important stock issue. Topicality as a voting issue is related to the case as a whole and requires that the entire case uphold the resolution. Topicality as a stock issue relates specific elements of the case to the resolution, particularly the definitions of the resolutional terms. Although the affirmative is required to incorporate every word of the resolution into its case by accomplishing the action required by the resolution, it does not have to explicitly define words such as *the*. Once the key terms are defined, the rest of the case must be consistent with the definitions.

TEACHER'S NOTE:

All elements of the affirmative case must stem from the resolution. Be certain that your team first of all roots the significant harm and inherence in the resolution by determining where the inherent problem lies in the area defined by the resolution. Next, the plan must institute the action called for in the resolution, and the advantages must be possible only through institution of the plan. The relationship between topicality and the other stock issues can be explained using the logical process of "residues," as explained on page 105 of the textbook.

2. Significance—The issue of significance highlights the affirmative's need to show a significant disparity between the current system and an ideal. The affirmative must give the audience a good reason to make the change it is proposing. Debaters should answer questions in the audience's mind that relate to "Why should I care?"

TEACHER'S NOTE:

▷ The form of significance differs according to the type of case being run by the affirmative team. Some cases will show qualitative significance, some will show quantitative significance, and some will show both.

▷▷ *Qualitative significance—Even though a small number of people may be affected by the harm, the effect of the harm on these people is so great as to demand a change.*

▷▷ *Quantitative significance—A great number of people are harmed, or a large degree of some aspect of society is harmed. Sometimes only numbers will win a round, so whenever possible, quantify even the qualitative harms in the case.*

3. Inherence—This stock issue is usually the one that gives the most intellectual challenge. Inherence argues that the harm will not go away on its own; there is some kind of barrier (either attitudinal, structural, or existential) in the present system that prevents the problem from being solved.

TEACHER'S NOTES:

▷ The affirmative must clearly link inherence to some resolutional element of the present system (the status quo) in order to fulfill its burden of proof. In other words, if the affirmative argues that we should change the status quo in the way the resolution suggests, then the reason for change must be tied to the area of the status quo that the resolution addresses.

▷ In policy debate, this is the most difficult of the stock issues for a student to grasp. Inherence is sometimes explained as "blame"—who is to blame for the problem? In the process of assessing the blame, the debater shows that the guilty party will not or cannot change the problem. Others explain that inherence is the "link" between the harm and the current system. It is a barrier (either structural or existential or attitudinal) that prevents any solution to the harm until something is changed. For instance, the sin nature is an inherent human problem.

EXERCISE:

Choose two or three examples of current problems in society and ask your debaters to identify the inherent elements of the problem. For instance, you might use the problem of health care costs. Of the numerous factors that contribute to the high cost of health care in the U.S. (physicians' insurance premiums, malpractice lawsuits, advanced research and development, state-of-the-art technology, rising numbers of elderly people needing growing amounts of medical care, etc.), which of the contributing factors are inherent to the problem? That is, which factors will not go away until action is taken to remove them?

4. Solvency—Solvency encompasses five specific areas of argumentation:

a) Presenting the plan—The plan consists of the affirmative's suggested change to the present system in order to solve the significant, inherent harm. The plan, which is discussed in Chapter 9 of the textbook, is usually composed of five "planks" that work together to provide the necessary action called for in the resolution. Presenting a plan that accomplishes the requirements of the resolutions is an element of topicality.

b) Solving the harm—The plan must also solve the harm presented earlier in the 1AC speech (the case). Once the affirmative has identified a significant, inherent reason to change, then its plan must solve those specific problems.

c) Proving workability—The affirmative plan must actually work to solve the significant, inherent problems in the present system.

TEACHER'S NOTE:

Sometimes workability is confused with the concept of fiat. Fiat is a convention adopted by debate theorists to avoid useless arguments about whether or not the government would actually adopt the plan. Instead, the goal of the debate is to decide whether the policy would solve the harm if it were adopted. In other words, fiat prevents the negative team from arguing that the affirmative plan would never happen. Fiat assumes that the plan would be implemented, enabling the discussion to stay focused on the merits of the idea. Workability, however, is a different matter. Workability means that the affirmative must show that when placed into effect, the plan can succeed—enough dollars and personnel have been allotted to the problem, it overcomes the barrier in the current system, etc. While affirmatives may claim fiat for actually putting the plan into place, they cannot fiat its workability. See Chapter 9 of the textbook.

---

d) Producing advantages—Advantages must arise from placing the plan into effect and thus solving the harm. Together, the plan and the advantages comprise the stock issue of solvency. Remember that an advantage must be developed as completely as harm contentions.

e) Causing no disadvantages—Affirmatives should also be prepared to show that no significant disadvantages will arise from the proposed change.

TEACHER'S NOTE:

Having some sense of what the opposition might do and how they might respond gives the affirmative team a lot of flexibility in the round, so help your debaters anticipate the criticisms of their case which might come from the negative team. This preparation will allow the affirmative team to specifically respond to any disadvantages the negative team may present against its case.

B. Incorporating stock issues into different case types

Types of affirmative cases other than the traditional plan-meet-need case also require that stock issues be incorporated into their development. Each of these case types is discussed in more detail in Chapter 9 of the textbook.

EXERCISE:

Help your students practice applying stock issues to everyday topics by having them respond to each question or statement which follows. Please note that the alternative justification format is not included because it is merely two or more minicases that use one of the other case formats.

▷ 1. Would it be better exercise to run a 5K race or to swim a mile three times a week? *(This question allows students to practice the thinking necessary for organizing a comparative advantages case.)*

▷ 2. We should require that U.S. schoolchildren learn Spanish as a second language. *(To evaluate this statement, students must organize their thinking as they would for a plan-meet-need case.)*

▷ 3. Your goal is to graduate from high school in three years so you can live abroad for a year before beginning college. Discuss how you can meet all of your graduation requirements on time. *(This example requires thinking about the topic in a manner consistent with the goals criteria organization.)*

II. STOCK ISSUES FOR VALUE DEBATE

Although both forms of debate include the same decision-making concepts, stock issues are organized differently in value debate than in policy debate because the manner in which a decision is made is somewhat different. In value debate, the traditional stock issues are restructured into two general value stock issues—definitive and designative issues, with subcategories within each. There is one additional concept added to value debate stock issues that is not present in policy stock issues: the value-criterion.

A. Definitive issue

The definitive issue includes the observations of definitions, the value, the criterion used to make the value judgment, and an optional resolutional analysis. These elements make it possible to understand the parameters of the debate round. In other words, these elements "define" the area within which the debate will take place.

TEACHER'S NOTES:

▷ Just as they do in policy debate, definitions set the context for a round of value debate.

▷ The criteria, sometimes called the value-criterion, is the key to value debate. The criteria links the whole case together, providing the source from which definitions, topicality, and contentions radiate. Your debaters will need you to help them in this area. Help them see that there must be a connection between the criteria and the definitions. Likewise, the criteria must be related to the real-world issues presented in the contentions.

    It is easy to use emotional arguments when talking about values that are important to us. Introducing the concept of the criterion in a round reduces the temptation to rely on emotional arguments and helps the debater to think about matters of importance in more objective terms. The criterion gives the judge and audience an objective way to determine if the affirmative value is being met or violated in the present system.

▷ Here is an example of a case that ties the criteria to both the definitions and the contentions:

  ▷▷ *Resolved: That the United States has inappropriately undermined civil rights in order to guarantee national security.* The question the affirmative debater had to answer was this: When does the loss of civil rights for the sake of national security become inappropriate?

  ▷▷ One affirmative team argued that when the loss of civil rights was necessary and defensible (as defined in the affirmative case), then the government action was appropriate. If a government action did not meet the criterion of being necessary and defensible, then such an action was inappropriate. The affirmative went on to show that the government had taken unnecessary and indefensible actions in the real world and had therefore inappropriately undermined the value of civil rights in order to guarantee national security.

  ▷▷ Note that the value-criterion presented was strongly tied to the definition of *inappropriate* by operationally defining that term through the criterion of necessary and defensible.

  ▷▷ Also note that the criterion was linked to the contentions: the contentions showed actions that were unnecessary and indefensible.

  ▷▷ The affirmative then needed only to take the final step of showing that by violating the criterion, the government violated the value of civil rights that the affirmative had chosen as the highest value in the round. The violation of the value is demonstrated as the *impact* of the contention.

EXERCISE:

Take this year's LD debate topic and discuss with your debaters how different values could be used to talk about the topic. When the value changes, the arguments change, and sometimes our decision changes.

B. Designative issue

The designative stock issue has two distinct aspects that contribute to its development: *correspondence* and *application*. Correspondence requires the affirmative contentions to address the value resolution as well as uphold the affirmative's own definitions and criteria. Application requires the affirmative contentions to show what happens when their value and criterion are applied to a real-world situation. The affirmative accomplishes correspondence and application through contentions that serve as examples both of how the affirmative value is presently being violated or upheld and of the harmful or beneficial effects (impact) of the real-world treatment of the value.

TEACHER'S NOTES:

▷ Contentions must show there are *significant* value violations that will occur if the resolution is not upheld. The contention must violate a value that is important to us, and the violation must create a significant harm (impact) in the round.

To show the value violation is *inherent,* the affirmative must prove that the harm is occurring in the present and is not going away. The case should therefore be argued in the verb tense that corresponds with the resolution.

Imagine that the affirmative is arguing that the Patriot Act violates the civil rights of U.S. citizens by allowing for surveillance of citizens for a period of time without notifying the individual of the surveillance. The negative might respond by arguing that the attorney general is a committed Christian who understands the importance of Americans' freedoms, and he would not allow any unnecessary infringement of this civil right. The problem, however, is that the attorney general serves at the pleasure of the current president, and the person staffing this position can change. Thus, the problem of value violation resides in the law, and we cannot depend upon an individual who can be replaced to protect us from the problem embedded in the law.

The *impact* of the value violation is the clincher of the argument. This is where the debater increases his persuasiveness by adding the human element to the round. The debater helps us see how this violation affects people like us, others we are responsible for, or aspects of the world for which we care. When the audience is able to personalize the effect of the value violation, it understands the case at a deeper level.

▷ Each contention written to show violation of the value should be independent, meaning that each contention wins or loses alone. It should not depend upon another contention to supplement its meaning.

▷ The concept of application provides a good opportunity to talk about the practicality of debate as a whole. Show your students how the skill of debate allows us to talk about real problems in an objective and organized manner so that there is opportunity to make the best possible decision.

III. STOCK ISSUES IN THE DEBATE ROUND

A. Prove the issue.
A successfully presented argument requires the debater to:
▷ specifically *address* the issue;
▷ *explain* the position her side of the resolution advances;
▷ *use evidence* to support her position; and
▷ *apply* the relevance and importance of her argument to the debate overall.

B. Win the affirmative case.
Affirmatives must win each stock issue, but not necessarily each argument in the debate. Remember that it is necessary to win one harm and one advantage in its totality.

C. Prepare the negative.
It is not possible, especially at the beginning of the season, to have arguments against all affirmative cases. Begin negative preparation by first developing arguments against your own affirmative case, then develop some "generic" argument blocks that defend the current system in general.

D. Use understandable language.
Debaters should refrain from casually referring to stock issues in the round without explaining those terms in a few words that a layperson can understand.

TEACHER'S NOTE:
Remember that the judge does not apply the concept for the debater. For instance, an affirmative debater making an inherence argument must:
▷ explain inherence,
▷ show how his position is supported by inherence, and
▷ explain to the judge how the establishment of inherence should affect the outcome of the debate.

A negative debater attacking the affirmative inherence argument must:

▷ *refute* the affirmative argument directly. In other words, the debater must specifically announce that he sees a fault in the affirmative inherence argument and explain what the fault is. Perhaps there is no link between the harm and the subject of the resolution, or perhaps the affirmative has linked the harm to the wrong source.

▷ *relate* the refutation of the specific affirmative argument (such as a harm) to the negative's overall view of inherence. The goal is to find something to blame other than the current system.

▷ *read* evidence to support the negative argument.

▷ *explain* to the judge how this argument should affect the outcome of the debate.

Please note that these steps can be used in conjunction with the three levels of relation found in Chapter 7 of the textbook.

E. Keep the right perspective.

A round of debate can be decided on an issue other than a stock issue. For instance, an off-case argument can be used to make the final decision in a round. In the end, each team is responsible only to do its best as it argues all the relevant issues in the round.

TEACHER'S NOTE:

It is important to remember that stock issue arguments are not magical arguments that require the judge to vote in a team's favor. Instead, stock issues are based upon common-sense theories crafted to help debaters address the *most common issues* that face the decision maker.

In policy debate, teams may face additional issues:

▷ Which team presented the best evidence

▷ Which team presented a more consistent case or position

▷ Minor repairs offered by the negative team

▷ Disadvantages that outweigh the advantages of the affirmative case

▷ Whether or not the affirmative carried a complete contention

In value debate, other issues may be a factor for the judge:[1]

▷ The formation of an appropriate value-criterion for judging fact and value claims: *What is significant for making this decision? Why?*

▷ The relative importance of various criterions

▷ Whether the evidence, values, and credibility produced are applicable to the criteria: *Are comparable things being compared? Is there too much bias on this question to trust the criteria it provides? Are proper values reflected?*

▷ The acceptability of the evidence, values, and credibility: *Are statistics accurate? Is the source trustworthy and competent? What value can we place on statistics as compared with what Scripture says?*

F. Convince the judge.

Debaters should use the last rebuttal speeches to help the judge see why they have won certain stock issues, if negative, or all of the stock issues, if affirmative. In addition, each side should point out how it has won other issues that are pivotal in the debate, as outlined above. It is important that the last two speeches in the round persuasively summarize how that side wants the judge to view the resolution.

EXERCISES:

Have *policy debaters* define the following terms in their own words:
▷ topicality
▷ qualitative significance
▷ quantitative significance
▷ attitudinal inherence
▷ structural inherence
▷ existential inherence
▷ solvency

Have *value debaters* define the following in their own words:
▷ definitive issue
▷ designative issue
▷ value
▷ criteria
▷ correspondence
▷ application

Outline 6 Endnote

[1] Richard D. Rieke and Malcolm O. Sillars, *Argumentation and the Decision Making Process*, 3d ed. (New York: HarperCollins College Publishers, 1993), 60.

7 Refutation and Rebuttal

I. DEFINITIONS OF REFUTATION AND REBUTTAL

Refutation is argumentation meant to overcome opposing evidence and reasoning by proving that it is false or erroneous. *Rebuttal* is argumentation meant to overcome opposing evidence and reasoning by introducing other evidence and reasoning that will destroy its effect.

DISCUSSION QUESTION:

What is the difference between refutation and rebuttal? *(Refutation aims to prove that an opponent's argument or evidence is false, whereas rebuttal aims to prove that an argument or evidence is insignificant.)*

II. PRINCIPLES OF REFUTATION AND REBUTTAL

A. Understanding the argument

A debater should be clear about what her opponent is saying and fully understand the context of each argument her opponent makes.

EXERCISE:

Give your debaters a relatively short editorial to analyze. Do not allow your debaters to critique the argument. Instead, have them outline the argument so they understand what the author is saying. Advanced students should be able to outline an argument in about twenty minutes; however, this exercise could take a few hours for beginners, so you may want to assign this exercise as homework for first-time debaters or walk them through the process in class. Good places to look for editorials are your local paper, www.nytimes.com, www.drudgereport.com, or any other news website.

B. Determining how to approach the argument

1. Refuting evidence with evidence—Debaters should refute evidence with evidence in almost every situation.

2. Refuting reasoning with reasoning—When debaters use reasoning to refute an argument, they focus on critiquing their opponent's entire argument.

3. Refuting evidence with reasoning—There are three situations when debaters could use reasoning to refute evidence:
> when the evidence commits a reasoning fallacy,
> when the evidence fails a test of evidence, or
> when the logical conclusion of the evidence would produce more harm than good.

TEACHER'S NOTE:

"What do I do if I don't have evidence to refute my opponent's case?" is the most common question debaters ask about refutation. Your students are likely to face such a scenario, especially in the beginning of the season. Here are several strategies for overcoming this situation:
> In the beginning of the season, a lack of evidence on your debaters' part is often offset by the fact that their opponent's case is underdeveloped at this point, leaving it vulnerable to a solvency, inherence, and/or significance attack from your evidence-challenged debaters.
> Since the refutation strategy of discrediting an argument does not always require evidence, your debaters could discredit an argument by casting doubt in the audience's mind about the validity of the opponent's argument or evidence. Doing this can be risky, but then again, everything is risky when you have little or no evidence to refute an opponent's arguments. This strategy is discussed in detail later in this chapter.
> **Affirmative** debaters who do not have evidence to refute the negative's disadvantages or advantages should focus on rebuilding their affirmative case to show how the harms or advantages of their case are significant, how the plan is solving the harms, and how the plan is providing for certain advantages. If possible, these debaters should focus the debate on whether or not the claimed disadvantages of the negative are a sufficient reason to choose not to eliminate the harms. The debate then comes down to the audience weighing whether solving the harms would be better than the disadvantages that may occur.
> Arguing with little evidence when on the **negative** side is much more difficult. With little evidence against the affirmative case, the negative should focus on the areas of the case where reasoning can be effectively used. The stock issues are a good place for negatives to start. The debate round can be won by finding an affirmative reasoning error that damages or destroys at least one stock issue.

When short on evidence, the negative can address the stock issue of *inherency* by questioning whether the barrier is really so large that the affirmative plan is necessary. Or, the negative can always focus on whether the harms or advantages are *significant* as well as on the quantitative and qualitative impacts of those harms. (For an explanation of quantitative and qualitative harms, see Chapter 8 of the textbook.) If the impacts are not qualitative or quantitative, the negative should question if the harm really exists. After all, if something is truly harmful, then we should be able to see its negative consequences in real life. Without a demonstration of the real consequences, we have little reason to be concerned with the harm.

Attacking the stock issue of *solvency* is one of the easiest attacks for the negative to make because it simply questions if the plan will work. Attacking the workability of the plan, particularly the funding, is the easiest solvency argument to make. If the affirmative requires additional funding, the negative should question if the funding will be enough, particularly how we will know it is enough. Without enough money to fund the plan, the plan will not work.

Using the four levels of analysis described in Chapter 10 of the textbook will help negatives learn to spot stock issue weaknesses in affirmative cases.

C. Relating the argument to the big picture

1. Three levels of relation

a) Relate to your opponent's argument—When answering an argument, a debater should make sure to explicitly reference the exact point he is answering.

b) Relate to the stock issues—If a particular argument is not related to a stock issue, then it is probably not pivotal to the round. Debaters should take care to explicitly relate their refutation to an important issue in the round, and the stock issues are likely to be the most important issues.

c) Relate to the resolution—Debaters cannot stop at merely relating an argument to a stock issue. They must go one very important step further and explicitly relate each argument to the resolution itself.

I (Jeff) have sat in countless rounds where neither side of the debate related its arguments to the resolution. Many times, the debaters later realized that if they had simply related their opponent's arguments to the resolution, they would have won. Why? Because their opponent's arguments did not show a direct connection to the resolution.

2. Three benefits of relation

a) Provides clarity—Following the three levels of relation will automatically clarify the important issues for the debate round.

b) Establishes organization—The three levels of relation will allow debaters to organize their opponent's arguments into their own refutation and organize their speeches around the most important issues in the round.

TEACHER'S NOTES:

▷ When a student's refutation and rebuttal are focused on the stock issues, he is most likely to keep his remarks centered on the most important issues in the round. *Topicality* ensures that the debate is focusing on the topic that the debaters have worked hard to research. *Significance* requires that either the harms are significant (plan-meet-need, alternative justification, or goals criteria) or the advantages are significant (comparative advantage). *Inherence* requires that there be a connection between the significant problem and the area of the status quo that needs to be changed according to the resolution. *Solvency* ensures that all of the harms are really being solved in the plan or counterplan.

▷ Remember also to teach your students that they should organize their speeches in a way that builds to an overall rejection (or affirmation) of the resolution. Debaters should never take for granted that the judge will understand how a stock issue argument impacts the resolution; rather, they must explicitly state the connection.

▷ Emphasize the importance of clarity and organization in your students' arguments. Debaters many times think they are being clear when they are not. Teaching your debaters to use questions like *why*, *how*, and *so what* will enable them to adequately explain what they are saying. *Why* forces them to explain the reason for presenting that particular counterargument; *how* requires them to explain how the counterargument corresponds to their opponent's argument; and *so what* ensures that they explain why the audience should care about the counterargument by showing how the argument affects the resolution and debate round as a whole.

When your students are engaged in practice debates or are discussing arguments in class, interrupt them to ask *how*, *why*, and *so what* if they have not adequately explained their arguments. Continue to ask these three questions until they have adequately explained themselves. A student will often respond to your questioning by saying, "I was assuming that I didn't need to say that." Such an assumption is often fatal to her argument, resulting in the audience not understanding why that argument is important.

At times, asking these three questions may be tedious, but it will help your debaters in the end. Eventually, they will begin seeing their weaknesses and learn to explain themselves more fully. Once they begin to naturally answer these three questions in their explanations, you will notice a drastic improvement in the clarity and organization of their arguments. Be patient. This is a slow process that may be frustrating for your students, but it is better for them to be frustrated in class as part of the learning process than to be frustrated in the debate round because the judge voted against unclear, disorganized arguments.

---

c) Prevents fallacies—Reasoning fallacies are faulty argument structures that usually exist because the arguer has not taken the argument far enough. Fallacies usually say *that* something is right or wrong without saying *why* or *how* something is right or wrong.

TEACHER'S NOTES:

▷ Many instructors teach their students how to point out reasoning fallacies in others' arguments. It is even more beneficial, however, for students to learn to discern reasoning fallacies in their own arguments. In doing so, debaters can identify areas of weakness that they need to "look out for" when writing a debate case, writing a paper for a class, or talking with other people. As students learn to evaluate their own reasoning, they will in turn become better critical thinkers.

▷ Reasoning fallacies are not always fatal to an argument. They can often be remedied by stating and explaining assumptions in order to complete the argument. For example, the fallacy of a hasty generalization is based upon assumptions or other evidence that the speaker does not share with his audience or opponent. A simple explanation or use of additional evidence may clear up the reasoning and circumvent a fallacious argument.

▷ There are times when a reasoning fallacy cannot be corrected because it is structurally illogical. Make sure to explain to your students that simply stating that their opponent is committing a reasoning fallacy is not enough. They must go on to explain the faulty reasoning to the judge and show how the removal of the fallacy affects the round of debate. Otherwise, the audience does not know what the debaters want them to do.

FOR FURTHER STUDY:

The discussion that follows explores several of the common reasoning fallacies used in academic debate. For a more complete list of fallacies, see Christy Shipe's *An Introduction to Argumentation and Debate* or any logic textbook.

1. Hasty Generalization

   ▷ Definition: A fallacy of reasoning that occurs when we believe that what is true of the part is necessarily true of the whole.[1]
   ▷ Key Question: Has the evidence shown us a significant enough sampling to make us conclude that the whole affirmative or negative position is correct?
   ▷ Example: *Corporate emphasis on profit is excessive.* If the affirmative case gives an example of only one company that has excessively emphasized profit, has it really proved that the whole resolution is true?

2. False Dilemma

   ▷ Definition: A fallacy that occurs when the arguer presents an artificially restricted choice of two options. This kind of argument is a very simplistic way to look at a situation and is most often a choice between two extremes.
   ▷ Key Question: Why are these the only two options?
   ▷ Example: *Either we need to deport all illegal aliens or we need to have an open border.* This statement offers the extreme choice of keeping all aliens or getting rid of them all. Debaters should show that there are other options their opponent has not considered. It is rarely the case that there are only two solutions to a situation.

3. False Consolation

   ▷ Definition: A fallacy that uses an inappropriate analogy as a standard of quality.[2]
   ▷ Key Questions: Why are we making this comparison? What is the goal of using this analogy?
   ▷ Example: *Compared to the rest of the world, the poorest of Americans are wealthy.* If the purpose of this statement is to show that America is a wealthy nation, then the analogy is appropriate. If the purpose is to show that helping poor Americans is unnecessary, then the analogy is inappropriate. The fact that poor Americans are wealthier than citizens of other nations does not negate the responsibility of wealthy Americans to help the poor in their own country. Understanding the purpose of the analogy—how the analogy relates to the resolution—is crucial! Debaters must analyze whether the analogy actually supports or negates the resolution.

4. *Ad Populum*

   ▷ Definition: The fallacy that uses popularity as a standard of quality or as a proof of truth.
   ▷ Key Questions: If something is popular, does that mean it is true? What is the standard of truth or standard of measurement?
   ▷ Example: *Polling data.* Polling data is relevant if the question at hand is one of opinion. For example, if the question is what Americans think about gun control, then polling data that

reveals American opinion on this subject is logical. However, if the question at hand is one of fact or value, such as whether the president's "No Child Left Behind" education initiative is working to increase test scores, then polling data is irrelevant. The opinion of Americans does not determine whether or not a program is actually working. Truth is not determined by opinion. Just because a certain opinion is commonly accepted does not make it correct.

5. *Ad Hominem*

▷ Definition: A fallacy that occurs when we confuse the messenger with the message. In debate, this fallacy most often occurs when the debater attacks the qualifications or personal views of the individual in a way that is not connected with her argument.

▷ Key Question: How does the bias influence what is actually being said?

▷ Example: *The Sierra Club is very liberal, so we can't believe anything its members say.* Just because a particular group or author has conservative or liberal leanings does not make its position incorrect. If there is no evidence or reason to counter the substance of the argument, simply stating that "we can't listen to them because they are liberal (or conservative)" commits the fallacy of ad hominem. In order to properly question the bias of a source, debaters must link the bias to the substance of the arguments. See Chapter 3 of the textbook.

6. Non Sequitur

▷ Definition: A claim that is irrelevant to or unsupported by the evidence or premises purportedly supporting it.[3]

▷ Key Question: Does the evidence or reasoning actually prove the claim?

▷ Example: *My cousin died of cancer last year, so we know that the health care situation in this country is in trouble.* Once again, a fallacy has occurred because there is not enough explanation or connection between the evidence (my cousin died of cancer) and the claim (health care is in trouble). Spotting this fallacy requires debaters to listen carefully to what their opponents say and what evidence they read. Debaters should also carefully analyze their own evidence and reasoning to make sure it supports their arguments. See Chapter 3 of the textbook.

III. STRATEGIES OF REFUTATION AND REBUTTAL

Teaching your students strategies of refutation is less about giving them cookie-cutter responses to every possible argument and more about teaching them to ask good questions and think critically about any situation at any time.

A. Deny

To deny an argument is to claim the opposite of what the other team is arguing.

TEACHER'S NOTES:

▷ This particular strategy of refutation is most effective (1) when your debaters' evidence directly contradicts the other team's evidence or (2) when reasoning shows that the other team's argument is probably not logically accurate.

▷ The deny refutation strategy is a good place to start with your beginning debaters. This is the most natural thing for them to do when they are told that they must argue against someone else. After all, when they argue with their parents or a sibling, they are usually denying what their "opponent" is claiming.

▷ Since the deny strategy is closest to what they experience in life, it is often hard for debaters to use the other three refutation strategies. The best way to get your beginning debaters to use the three other refutation strategies is to help them "think their way out of a situation." In other words, force them to give you answers other than "you are wrong and I am right" to help them begin seeing alternatives. Once they begin seeing alternatives, then you can work with them on choosing the best alternative. Remember that your job isn't to know more information than your students, but simply to ask good questions that will enable them to learn how to think on their own.

EXERCISE:

Since beginners naturally use this refutation strategy, give an argument and require a response. You could use the following scenario to help your students begin to realize that they do not need to deny every argument in order to win the debate: *You want to go to a friend's house to spend the night, but your parents say that you have too much schoolwork to do. How do you convince your parents that you should be allowed to spend the night? The best strategy is not to tell your parents that they are wrong, but to show them how you will get your schoolwork done before going over to your friend's house.*

B. Discredit

To discredit an argument means to minimize its impact either by showing how it is not adequately supported by evidence or by showing that the source's bias calls the evidence into question.

TEACHER'S NOTES:

▷ Discrediting an argument is usually used (1) when the source of the evidence could contain potential bias which would inaccurately slant the evidence to a particular side or (2) when the evidence is correct but "doesn't tell the whole story."

▷ Debaters tend to want to claim that the other team's evidence is biased. The key is to remember that everyone is biased according to his or her own worldview. I am biased toward a Christian understanding of the world. I do not hide that bias, but it is important for others to know what my bias is because it affects every one of my thoughts and decisions. In the same way, we must understand how the bias of those with a completely different worldview affects how they view situations and thus the conclusions they reach. To blindly accept a source because of "expertise" without regard to the author's worldview is therefore dangerous. We should not summarily discount his expertise or dismiss his opinions, but we should take care to understand how his underlying worldview is influencing his argument. For example, when evaluating evidence from a group whose members do not believe God exists, we should keep their atheistic worldview in mind and understand how their atheism influences their argument. Otherwise, we might be tempted to blindly embrace their conclusions. Critical thinkers never heedlessly accept what anyone says; rather, they carefully examine statements so that they can unveil truth.

▷ Another popular way to discredit an argument is to point out that the other team is presenting a false dilemma—a reasoning fallacy that occurs when the arguer presents an artificially restricted choice of two options. Unfortunately, debaters often get caught up in the mindset that "they must defend everything at all costs." This mindset usually leads to presentation of a false dilemma.

C. Devalue

When a debater devalues an argument, she shows how the argument has little relevance or impact on the issues in the debate.

TEACHER'S NOTES:

▷ Devaluing the impact of an individual argument is a very effective strategy to use when the opponent picks very isolated instances to prove his point.

▷ Whereas discrediting an argument focuses on the evidence, devaluing an argument focuses on the reasons the audience should care that the impact of the argument exists. Your debaters should show how a few instances cannot be the cause for accepting or rejecting a resolution. The audience will find it hard to accept or reject a resolution if your debaters show that their opponents' arguments have little impact on the resolution.

▷ Devaluing the argument agrees that the evidence is true but asks why the audience should care by questioning the impact of the argument upon the debate. Impact points will usually talk about the number of people dying or hurt because of the current system (affirmative claim) or because of the affirmative plan (negative claim). If the impact of an argument claimed that people would die as a result of the opponent's case (affirmative or negative), your debaters would question if the impact matters. Although it is not good if even one or two people have died or been harmed, sometimes the numbers do not justify making changes. In essence, devaluing the argument asks the opponent to more adequately show why the audience should care (the *so what* question). Without a reason to care, a judge will not vote for that side.

DISCUSSION QUESTION:

What is the difference between discrediting and devaluing an argument? *(Discrediting an argu-ment emphasizes questioning the credibility of the evidence or reasoning that supports an argument. Devaluing an argument assumes that the evidence or reasoning is correct but shows how the argument itself makes little difference when applied to the resolution.)*

D. Dissolve

An argument is dissolved in one of two ways: either by eliminating the rele-vance of the argument to the debate or by flipping an opponent's argument in favor of the debater's own position.

DISCUSSION QUESTION:

What is the difference between devaluing an argument and dissolving an argument? *(Devaluing an argument means that the debater proves it has little or questionable relevance to the debate, whereas dissolving an argument means that the debater proves that the argument has no rele-vance to the debate at all. Dissolving an argument can also be accomplished by flipping an oppo-nent's argument to support the debater's own position.)*

FOR FURTHER STUDY:

▷ Joseph Corcoran developed a four-point method of refutation that can supplement the concepts taught in this chapter.[4] He suggests that to refute an argument clearly, the debater should:

1. point out which of the opponent's arguments he is refuting;

2. give a response to the argument, usually with only a sentence or two;

3. offer evidence supporting his own argument; and then

4. emphasize the impact of his argument against the opponent's.

▷ Have your students use Corcoran's four points of refutation in conjunction with one of the four strategies of refutation (deny, discredit, devalue, or dissolve). His method will give your debaters a good way to structure their refutation, ensuring that they read evidence against their oppo-nent's argument.

▷ Here is an example of what the four points of refutation would look like in practice:

1. "They say in the first point of their second harm that religious groups will influence legislators to enact federal legislation to suit their own religious preferences."

2. "We say that the federal courts would strike down any legislation that forces Americans to adopt the theological views of any particular religion."

3. "J. Philip Wogaman, professor of Christian Social Ethics at Wesley Theological Seminary, agreed with us in *The American Academy of Political and Social Science Annals* in November 1979 when he stated: 'And religious groups, when they go lobbying for (their own theological views) must expect them to be struck down eventually by the courts even if they are enacted into law.'"

4. "The impact of this evidence is that our government has checks and balances, and the courts would rein in any unconstitutional acts of the legislature." (Debaters would go on to state the impact upon the resolution or upon the debate as a whole.)

▷ These four points of refutation mesh well with the three levels of relation outlined earlier in this chapter, and the two methods can be used in conjunction with one another. The first three points of refutation generally correspond with the first level of relation (relate your argument to your opponent's argument), and the fourth point of refutation corresponds with the second and third levels of relation (relate to the stock issues and to the resolution to show the impact of the argument).

EXERCISE:

Read an affirmative harm or negative disadvantage and give your students one minute to prepare an argument against the harm or disadvantage. Require them to use one of the four strategies of refutation, structuring their arguments according to the four points of refutation and addressing all three levels of relation. Then, assign a different strategy of refutation to each person in the group and repeat the exercises. Students should practice using all of the strategies until they are comfortable with them and could readily apply them to arguments in the debate round.

Chapter 7 Endnotes

[1] B. Hill and R. W. Leeman, *The Art and Practice of Argumentation and Debate* (Mountain View, CA: Mayfield Publishing Company, 1997), 346.

[2] Ibid., 96.

[3] E. S. Inch and B. Warnick, *Critical Thinking and Communication: The Use of Reason in Argument*, 3d ed. (Needham Heights, MA: Allyn and Bacon, 1998), 162–63.

[4] Joseph Corcoran, *An Introduction to Non-policy Debating* (Dubuque, IA: Kendall/Hunt, 1988), 29.

8 Advancing and Advocating the Affirmative

OUTLINE

I. SELECTION OF THE AFFIRMATIVE ADVOCACY

A. Choosing advocacy that is central to the topic

Preparation of the affirmative case begins with thorough research of the topic. After examining and evaluating the evidence, debaters should choose a case *area* that will directly affirm the resolution and choose a case *type* that will effectively communicate the evidence. A case that directly affirms the resolution offers the affirmative two distinct advantages:

1. The advantage of preparation—A direct case leads to more predictable negative responses, making the affirmative's job easier.

2. The advantage of topicality—Topicality arguments are an advantage of the negative team that the affirmative can avoid by not arguing a "surprise" case.

B. Nailing down the stock issues

1. Significance—Debaters should try to establish both qualitative and quantitative harms.

2. Inherency—Debaters can protect their cases against negative inherency attacks by writing a plan that directly changes both the significant harms of the current system and the structures or attitudes embedded in the current system.

3. Solvency—The case should offer a workable solution to the problems of the current system.

TEACHER'S NOTE:

No judge will vote for a case that he believes will fail, so the affirmative case must be workable. Because the current system is "presumed innocent until proven guilty," there is no reason for the judge to condemn the current system (and thereby vote for the affirmative team) unless "guilt" has been proven and the benefits of a new, workable plan have been established. In the case of a tie, the judge will award the win to the negative, as explained in Chapters 5 and 6.

EXERCISE:

Assign a hypothetical resolution to the debaters, such as *Resolved: That computer games decrease student achievement.* Have the students:
▷ define the key terms of the resolution,
▷ identify the assumptions of the resolution, and
▷ develop at least three lines of argument that emerge from each assumption.

II. PERSUASION IN SPECIFIC AFFIRMATIVE SPEECHES

Each affirmative speech presents unique challenges and opportunities for the affirmative speakers. As these debaters learn about the many different elements of each affirmative speech, they should consistently focus on the arguments and strategies that will most directly affirm the resolution and strengthen their case.

A. First affirmative constructive

The rhetorical purpose of the 1AC is to convincingly introduce the affirmative's case and gain the judge's sympathy for the affirmative plan. For more information on case construction, see Chapter 9.

B. Second affirmative constructive

The 2AC is the most important affirmative speech because it is the only affirmative speech that may introduce original argumentation.

TEACHER'S NOTE:

About half of this chapter discusses the 2AC, indicating how important this speech is in the round. However, the foundation of the 2AC is the case presented in the 1AC; the whole affirmative position is only as strong as that foundation. Therefore, it is crucial for both affirmative debaters to work on their case together and know the case well.

When assigning the second affirmative position to the debaters, first consider who knows the case the best. The debater who spends the most time writing the case often knows the case best and wants to be the person to premier the case. This, however, is not usually the best coaching decision. Instead, consider placing the student who wrote the case in the 2AC position so that the case can be most effectively explained and developed for the judge, especially if the other member of the team is not very familiar with the case.

1. Extending affirmative arguments—The 2AC should extend each argument presented in the original case, using the same outline presented in the 1AC. Extensions force the 1NC to spend more of his time refuting on-case arguments instead of presenting off-case arguments. Good extensions in the 2AC also better prepare the 1AR to refute the negative by enabling him to focus on on-case arguments instead of having to refute off-case arguments.

TEACHER'S NOTE:

An extension is a new implication of the argument. Debate scholar M. Sproule asserts, "When an argument has been refuted, one cannot merely repeat the argument. . . . In essence, to extend an argument gives it new substance and force. It follows, therefore, that effective resubstantiation extends a line of argument, forcing the opposition to spend time dealing with it. When one extends the line of argument, one wins the point, pending further debate."[1] In other words, an extended argument is able to win the point because it answers previous counterarguments, whereas an argument that is simply repeated fails to defeat an opponent's attack.

EXERCISE:

The week after the 1AC speeches are due, have your teams work with you to build the structure of the 2AC extensions. These extensions should (1) develop each issue more fully; (2) expand arguments made in the 1AC with new evidence and, more importantly, new reasons to support the original arguments; and (3) preempt expected negative attacks by initiating a positive argument that supports the affirmative case and at the same time refutes an expected negative argument. Sometimes a preemptive attack by the affirmative discourages the negative from making the argument altogether. If negatives still make the argument, it will carry less weight with the judge because the affirmative argument has inoculated the judge against the negative idea. You can help your debaters by proposing objections against the case that the second speaker may need to answer in a debate round.

2. Preparing a defense against general negative attacks—Affirmative teams can often anticipate the most common negative arguments against their cases. Debaters should spend time brainstorming possible negative arguments and then do the following:

a) Research against the 1AC—Debaters must spend time looking at evidence that opposes their case in order to arm themselves with evidence that will answer opposing positions.

b) Prepare evidence blocks—The evidence they find to support their position against opposing evidence should be organized into blocks.

EXERCISE:

Guide your debaters as they prepare a list of case areas and anticipated negative attacks. Then divide the work load by having each debater prepare evidence blocks to answer a specific number of anticipated negative attacks. Students can later share their prepared evidence blocks. A sample evidence block is provided at the end of this chapter outline.

---

3. Answering specific negative attacks

a) Topicality—This is one of two of the most dangerous attacks the negative can make against the affirmative (the other is a prima facie challenge).

(1) General topicality—The affirmative can answer general topicality attacks by either of the following two methods:

(a) Defeating the negative's interpretations, or

(b) Meeting the negative's interpretations.

(2) Extratopicality—Some components of the affirmative case should *not* fall outside the resolution, while other extratopical components may be allowed.

(a) Extratopical plan planks—Plan planks should be topical and stay within the boundaries of the resolution. Funding and enforcement are considered an integral part of any policy resolution, even if they are not explicitly mentioned in the resolution itself.

(b) Extratopical advantages—Extratopical advantages that occur as a natural result of topical plan planks are legitimate advantages of the affirmative case. Advantages that occur because of funding or enforcement plan planks are generally *not* considered legitimate unless the resolution explicitly calls for a certain type of funding or enforcement.

(3) **Subtopicality**—Negatives usually argue that the affirmative has not instituted a *significant* or a *substantial* change as called for in the resolution.

b) **Solvency**—Negatives can attack solvency in one of three ways: by directly attacking the affirmative plan, by offering disadvantages that would outweigh any advantages of the affirmative plan, or by offering their own nontopical counterplan to solve the problem (or accomplish the goal) identified in the affirmative case.

(1) **Direct plan attacks**—There are four ways to answer a direct negative attack on the plan:

(a) **Empirical evidence**—This type of evidence always provides the most effective defense.

(b) **Results of a study**—Most people are willing to accept the results of a study as good evidence that a plan would work.

(c) **Opinion of an expert**—The testimony of an expert is often an acceptable way to substantiate the workability of a plan.

(d) **Analogy to similar programs**—If there is no direct evidence regarding the plan, an analogy to a similar program previously adopted by a single state or by a foreign country can help show that the plan would work.

(2) **Disadvantages**—Negative teams often argue that the disadvantages of the affirmative plan far outweigh any advantages, thus making the plan worse than the present system. The affirmative has eleven ways to answer such claims.

(a) Link turn—The affirmative claims that the plan does the opposite of what the negative claims.

(b) Impact turn—The affirmative argues that the outcome of the supposed disadvantage is positive rather than negative.

(c) No link—The affirmative argues that there is no link between the plan and the disadvantage.

(d) Empirical denial—The affirmative presents evidence to show that the same plan enacted in the past did not cause the disadvantages alleged by the negative.

(e) Nonunique—The affirmative argues that factors other than the plan contribute to or cause the same disadvantage. In other words, the disadvantage is not inherent to the affirmative plan.

(f) No impact—The affirmative denies that the disadvantage has any significant impact upon the plan.

(g) No brink—The affirmative argues that the plan does not push society over the brink into some kind of disadvantage.

(h) No internal link—The affirmative argues that the negative has failed to prove all of the necessary links between the plan and the disadvantage.

(i) No threshold—The affirmative questions the validity of the disadvantage by showing that there is no way to measure how much action will lead to the impacts of the disadvantage.

(j) No timeframe—The affirmative shows that there is no way to know when the disadvantage would occur; it could occur in the distant future and is therefore not a reason to reject the affirmative plan.

(k) No scenario—The affirmative forces the negative to give a real-life example of the supposed disadvantage.

(3) Counterplans—The negative will sometimes run a nontopical counterplan that competes directly with the affirmative plan for the judge's vote. In such cases, the negative loses presumption. There are three strategies for answering a counterplan:

(a) Permutation—The affirmative argues that if both plans could be adopted, the judge should vote affirmative.

TEACHER'S NOTE:

The concept of permutation requires that the negative present a counterplan that is mutually exclusive of the affirmative plan (rather than completely outside of the resolution). This situation is not as likely to occur in NCFCA, because NCFCA resolutions are usually written very broadly. It would therefore be very difficult for the negative team to solve the affirmative harms outside of the resolution.

(b) Solvency—The affirmative argues that the negative counterplan does not solve the harms identified by the affirmative or accomplish the affirmative's goal as effectively as its own plan.

(c) Disadvantages—These are similar to the negative disadvantages discussed in Chapter 10.

EXERCISE:

Create several negative arguments, taking them from your flow sheets of previous debates or from ideas generated in class or during online discussions of the debate topic. When the class meets, place members into groups of two. Have them practice making affirmative responses to the negative solvency attacks and negative disadvantages that you have prepared by having one debater argue the affirmative position and the other, the negative. Students should use one of the hints given in the chapter to make each affirmative defense. Have each duo switch sides and repeat the exercise.

C. First affirmative rebuttal

This is the most difficult speech in debate. It requires a combination of persuasion skills, issue-selection skills, word economy, and passion. The 1AR must both win back the arguments in the round and win the heart of the judge.

1. Build upon the 2AC—Since speakers are not allowed to bring new arguments into rebuttal speeches, the 1AR should focus on synthesizing the arguments already presented by the 2AC.

2. Extend the important arguments—The job of the 1AR is to boil the debate down to several key issues that the affirmative can win.

TEACHER'S NOTE:

The important arguments are the ones that are most likely to influence the judge's decision. The affirmative speaker can have some influence on the decision by emphasizing particular arguments as the ones that are important to policy makers and experts. The speaker should begin by emphasizing the arguments that the affirmative team has chosen as its strongest arguments. She should then choose arguments that are centered on the affirmative theme for the round. Following this procedure will benefit the 2AR.

3. Read minimal evidence—With only five minutes to speak, the 1AR should focus on summarizing arguments rather than on reading lots of evidence.

TEACHER'S NOTE:

One exception to the general rule of reading minimal evidence is when a piece of evidence has been in dispute. In that situation, the 1AR should reread the evidence. Remember, the judge is probably not as familiar with the evidence as the competing teams are; this time, knowing the evidence is in contention, he can perhaps listen to it more carefully than he did the first time.

4. Win back the judge—Focus on the person deciding the debate. The 1AR should be careful to explain to the judge why the affirmative arguments are important to the debate and to the judge personally.

TEACHER'S NOTE:

After a few months, debaters will often get to know some of the judges that are volunteering at their tournaments. If the debaters know what judging paradigm a particular judge applies in a round, then their rebuttals can begin to emphasize arguments in light of the rules they predict the judge will employ. The debaters can also apply basic rules of audience analysis in reference to the judge. Gender, education level, age, race, etc., should be taken into account when making appeals that might engage the judge personally. Perhaps, for instance, the debater can effectively appeal to an argument for patriotism if he knows a judge has served in the armed forces.

EXERCISE:

Word economy is an important skill for any public speaker, and especially so for a debater. As you listen to one of your debaters speak, determine whether he is concisely explaining his position. (If possible, actually time the student.) When the student finishes speaking, ask him to tell you the same thing again but to use fewer words and less time. The goal is to help the student become conscious of how many words he uses to express an idea and to trim the words without robbing the idea of important detail or psychological impact. You can help him learn to read nonverbal cues at the same time by instructing him to watch for signals you might give that you understand and want him to go on, or that you are confused and need more detail, or that he is making a good point and should drive it home. Repeat this exercise frequently to give your debaters extensive practice with word economy.

D. Second affirmative rebuttal

If the affirmative has been doing its job throughout the debate round, it will have presented a complete (prima facie) case for change in the 1AC, set a solid foundation for the rest of the round in the 2AC, and used the 1AR to pivot the debate in its favor after the negative block. Now it is time for the grand slam in the 2AR.

1. Guidelines for an effective 2AR—Although some debaters exaggerate the truth at this point in the debate, there are several ethical ways for the 2AR to make a powerful speech without compromising the truth.

a) Outline the 2AR before the 1AC—The affirmative should know from the beginning what the essential points will be at the end of the debate round.

TEACHER'S NOTE:

Affirmatives should know what arguments they must carry in order to be able to win the round of debate. Once they have determined the essential arguments, perhaps with your input, they will be ready to discuss how to present the 2AR. If, as the chapter states, these arguments have been highlighted in the 2AC and the 1AR, the last speaker's job will be much easier. It is important for your students to understand that this is not a preplanned (or "canned") speech; it cannot be memorized ahead of time and delivered. Instead, the speaker secures a general understanding of what will need to be covered in order to meet the goals of the team and to reinforce the theme of the case. It is important to remember the skills listed for the 1AR and employ those skills here also. Those skills cannot be exhibited unless the speech is delivered extemporaneously—that is, well-thought-out but not memorized. This speech will differ somewhat from one affirmative round to another, based on the arguments that have been made by both teams.

b) Win the judge, not the flowsheet—Affirmatives should remember that they are speaking to a person and not just outlining arguments on paper.

TEACHER'S NOTE:

The goal of the 2AR—and of all debate speeches—is to convince the judge of the correctness of the debater's position. It should not be the debater's goal to impress the judge with how smart or how fluent he is. The team with the better arguments is not necessarily the team with the most impressive speaking skills. The ideal, of course, is for debaters to aim to employ fluent speaking skills as they concentrate on convincing the judge of the substance of their arguments. Remember that Aristotle taught pathos as an essential element of persuasion, but one that was secondary to logos. Debaters should allow logos (reason, fact, truth) to guide their use of pathos (emotional appeal) and never allow pathos to become the guiding principle of their speeches.

Likewise, debaters should concentrate on the substance of what they are saying and not focus on trying to elevate themselves in the mind of the judge. Debate is not a popularity contest but a trial of ideas. You might need to help your debaters keep their perspective here. No one likes to listen to a know-it-all, especially a wet-behind-the-ears know-it-all! Human nature tempts us to try to impress with our well-honed skills. But what is necessary in persuasion is for the listener to understand the argument being made and to desire to accept the argument that is best.

c) Don't go for everything—The 2AR should focus on those issues that are critical for the affirmative to win.

DISCUSSION QUESTION:

What are the critical issues? *(Those that support your theme or goal; those that weaken arguments introduced by the negative; and those that carry psychological wallop—whether positive or negative.)*

2. Mechanics of the 2AR—Debaters should have a basic structure of the last affirmative speech prepared in advance and then adapt their remarks to the specific negative arguments advanced in the round.

a) Off-case issues—The 2AR should begin with topicality if necessary, then move on to other substantive issues that have been introduced by the negative, such as the negative philosophy and the disadvantages.

b) On-case issues—This speaker should save the strongest arguments for the end of the speech in order to increase the persuasive effect of the presentation. This strategy also allows for a strong summary of the affirmative case at the end of the speech.

TEACHER'S NOTE:

Throughout the speech, the 2AR should address the most damaging negative attacks in one last attempt to weaken them and should address the strongest affirmative arguments in an attempt to leave a strong final impression.

EXERCISE:

To give your debaters practice with their 2AR speeches, select two or three negative arguments against the affirmative case that each student must answer. If time allows, have each speaker give a second 2AR speech so that students have an opportunity to incorporate your constructive criticism. Vary the negative attacks the speaker must answer in his second speech so that he cannot give the same speech in the same way. Emphasize that the goal is not to memorize the final speech but to learn to move smoothly through the negative attacks while defending the case theme and important elements of the case.

FOR FURTHER STUDY:

The one speech area that this text does not specifically address is cross-examination. The following information is therefore provided to assist your efforts to teach this skill to your debaters in both policy and value debate.

Although some accuse cross-examination debate of putting a premium on glibness, the cross-examination periods do require debaters to be thoroughly prepared and adjust their ideas rapidly to new situations. Cross-examination debate also reduces misunderstanding of terms used, presents more opportunity for a clash of ideas, and draws the audience into the debate by exciting their interest.

The purpose of the questioning period is to clarify issues and to expose the weaknesses of the opponent's case. Both the questioner and the witness should observe the rules of platform decorum and not allow the debate to bog down in a mire of confused wrangling and quibbling. Both speakers should take special care to be courteous during cross-examination. During the questioning period, neither the questioner nor the witness should receive aid from his partner. The questioner should stand near the center of the speaking area.

Professor Crocker in *Argumentation and Debate* points out that the questioning period is the heart of cross-examination debate and that careful consideration should be given to the question of what issues to cross-examine. He gives suggestions from Aristotle's *Rhetoric* (1419a): "Cross Examination is most effective when your opponent (a) has admitted so much that one more question lays bare his absurdity; (b) has to admit some premise to your conclusion and the other premise is obvious; (c) must contradict either himself or what his hearers generally hold to be true; and (d) must resort to equivocal answers such as 'Yes and no,' and 'Partly yes and partly no,' or 'In one sense, yes; in another sense, no.'"[2]

Professor Hance lists the following nine suggestions for improving one's skill in drawing out material that is damaging to the opponent's case and helpful to one's own:

1. Let your questioning period be such as to draw out your opponent. Inquire rather than tell.

2. Win your opponents and your audience by avoiding a belligerent attitude. Do not be a know-it-all.

3. Do not interrupt your opponent. If your question has not been asked so that it can be answered with yes or no, do not appear unfair by stopping your opponent.

4. By being good-natured, the examiner can turn the ill nature of his opponent to his own favor in the eyes of his audience.

5. The examiner should be quick to point out in his next speech how the reluctance or silence of the respondent redounds to his own benefit.

6. After arriving at a series of admissions, the examiner would show in her team's next speech how these admissions support the major assumptions of her case.

7. The examiner should get the opposition to admit analogies that apparently have nothing to do with the premise under consideration and at the proper moment show how the admitted analogies have a striking similarity to the proposition that he is seeking to establish.

8. The question should be on an apparently inconsequential matter, the answer to which will in reality damage the case of the opposition when synthesized.

9. The questions should lead up to the admission of a premise that leads to the substantiation of one's own case.[3]

The specific guidelines for questioners and responders in this form of debate can be summarized as follows.

For the questioner:

1. Ask fair questions that have a direct bearing on the debate as it has developed.

2. Your time must be confined to questions. You are not to make comments, make statements, or argue with the witness.

3. The questioning period is under your control. You may interrupt the witness and request shorter or more direct answers.

For the witness:

1. Answer briefly and directly all fair and relevant questions.

2. Do not question or argue with the questioner.

3. Do not give unduly long answers.

4. Do not evade fair questions or refuse to answer.

5. You may refuse to answer tricky or irrelevant questions if you state your reason for doing so.

Like every tool, cross-examination has its limitations. For one thing, it is a real challenge to frame a series of concise, pointed questions that get at the important issues, especially so for the novice debater. It can also invite the tendency to quibble over terms, ask personal or otherwise irrelevant questions, and show off or playact. When used properly, though, cross-examination debate is a powerful facilitator of exciting argumentation.

Sample Evidence Block

This sample evidence block was prepared for the affirmative to support a case that would eliminate the federal personal income tax and replace it with a national sales tax. Note that the block contains evidence on one topic from many different angles so that the affirmative is able to choose the piece that would best answer a specific negative attack.

DEBT—harms

U.S. Government is practically bankrupt:
Robert W. Haseltine, *USA Today Magazine*, May 1994, v122 n2588, p17
"According to some very reliable sources in the private sector, the nation has reached a point where even a balanced budget is not going to help its economic plight very much. Because of the total debt and the amount that automatically is earmarked for various programs already contracted for even before the budget is drawn up, it is virtually impossible for any debt reduction to occur. The U.S. has reached or passed the point of no return as far as the debt is concerned. The government, for all intents and purposes, is bankrupt."

Total taxes will be needed to pay just debt interest by 1997:
Robert W. Haseltine, *USA Today Magazine*, May 1994, v122 n2588, p17
"The crux of the problem is this: If the national debt increases at the rate it has

been these last few years, somewhere around the year 1997, the total tax revenue of the Federal government will be needed just to pay the interest on the debt. That situation already may be here, if the figures the government publishes are correct. That means the nation should be unable to go further in debt until it begins to pay off some of the old."

Dollar value has fallen because of debt:
Judy Shelton, *Washington Post*, Editorial, September 6, 1995, A21
"In the last decade, the dollar has plunged against the Japanese yen and the German mark. In April, it reached a post-World War II record low against both currencies: Compared with 1985, the dollar was worth 70 percent less in terms of the yen and 60 percent less with respect to the mark. . . . So long as the U.S. government runs a budget deficit and Americans rely on the savings of foreigners to fund domestic consumption, the downward pressure on the dollar will continue."

A considerable amount of our debt is owned overseas:
Robert W. Haseltine, *USA Today Magazine*, May 1994, v122 n2588, p17
"The major issue is not this, but one foisted on Americans over the past decade and a half—the ever-burgeoning national debt. This would not be so bad if it were owned within the limits of the U.S. economy. Until about 1988, such was the case. Little of the debt was owned overseas. This is not so anymore, as America now is a debtor nation with more than half its debt owned by other countries. This means they have a call on U.S. products and resources if they demand repayment."

Outline 8 Endnotes

[1] J. Michael Sproule, *Argument: Language and Its Influence* (New York: McGraw-Hill, 1980), 428–31.

[2] Lionel Crocker, *Argumentation and Debate* (New York: American Book Company, 1944), 211.

[3] Kenneth G. Hance, "The Dialectic Method in Debate," *Quarterly Journal of Speech* 25:247, quoted in Crocker, *Argumentation and Debate*, 212.

9 Affirmative Case Structures

Choosing a case structure before researching the topic is a serious mistake because research enables debaters to learn how and why they will change the current system. Only after deciding the goal of the case should debaters choose a case structure.

TEACHER'S NOTE:

Students should not begin writing their affirmative case before they have sufficiently researched the topic. Before allowing them to write their affirmative case, have your students show you:

▷ why the current system needs to be changed,

▷ how they want to change it, and

▷ what the benefits/advantages are of adopting the affirmative plan.

I. COMPONENTS OF THE CASE

All case types have two things in common: definitions and the plan.

A. Definitions

Definitions provide the affirmative's interpretation of the resolution and help fulfill the stock issue of topicality. There are three factors that help debaters determine how to define the words of the resolution in the round: context, interpretation, and reasonableness.

1. Context—Debaters should carefully choose definitions that uphold the context in which the words of the resolution are used.

TEACHER'S NOTE:

Debaters should read the resolution with careful attention to the exact wording. The adjectives and adverbs are usually the most important words in identifying the context of the resolution.

These words identify the extent to which the current system must be changed. Phrases such as *substantially change* and *significantly reduce* should be carefully defined by the affirmative. Special attention should also be given to the exact tense of the verb(s) in the resolution.

2. Interpretation—Definitions must uphold the affirmative's interpretation of the resolution.

TEACHER'S NOTE:

Have your team identify the obvious topics that the resolution is dealing with as well as areas that are not easily recognizable. Some of the best affirmative cases are topics that are not "mainstream." If your debaters decide to go with a nonmainstream topic, be sure that their case still directly affirms the resolution, showing either a significant harm in the current system or a significant advantage over the current system.

3. Reasonableness—Definitions should offer a reasonable interpretation of the resolution as a whole.

TEACHER'S NOTE:

Help your debaters make sure their definitions are reasonable. The affirmative has the right to define the words of the resolution, but it is unreasonable and unethical for the affirmative to abuse this right by offering definitions that omit key parts, that are unreasonably narrow, or that are slanted in favor of the affirmative case in order to gain an unfair advantage. Negatives can easily defeat such interpretations by providing a more reasonable definition and explaining why the affirmative definition is not reasonable. If the negative team doesn't contest the affirmative's definitions, then the affirmative's definitions should be used because they are the only ones offered.

If the affirmative's definitions are reasonable, discourage your debaters from making negative arguments against the definitions. Many judges are easily frustrated by this type of pointless argument. Negatives should argue against definitions only if the affirmative is being abusive or nontopical.

B. The plan

The plan is the centerpiece of any policy debate because every aspect of the affirmative case filters through the plan. Presenting a workable plan is the first step in fulfilling the stock issue of solvency.

TEACHER'S NOTE:

The plan specifically outlines how the affirmative team will change the current system if its plan is adopted. In plan-meet-need, goals criteria, and alternative justification case structures, the plan serves as the link connecting the harms or failures in the current system with the advantages. In comparative advantage case structures, the plan is not solving for harms but rather offering significant advantages over the current system.

1. Methods of building a plan—There are four methods of building a plan:

a) Advocating a plan—Debaters can advocate a plan that someone else has previously suggested.

b) Combining plans—Debaters can combine a plan that someone has suggested with other plans.

c) Creating a unique plan—Debaters can create a plan that is completely unique.

d) Nationalizing a successful plan—Debaters can advocate a plan for the nation that has already succeeded at a state or regional level or that has succeeded in another country.

TEACHER'S NOTE:

Since the plan is the focal point of any policy debate, encourage your debaters to carefully research and think about their plans. A plan cannot be constructed until they know why a change needs to be made.

Encourage your debaters to begin constructing their plans by researching any existing plans proposed by members of Congress or already adopted at the state or local level. Starting with a plan that someone else has already constructed helps ease the load of research at the beginning of the case-writing process. However, debaters should not become lazy and adopt only plans that others have already created. Encourage your debaters to be creative and dream up new ways to change the current system or ways to refine the plans of others. This effort at creativity will assist them in their critical thinking development. At the same time, help your debaters focus on being realistic and adopting plans that directly affirm the resolution.

2. Plan planks—All plans should have the same five planks.

a) Agency—The branch of government that will enact the plan.

TEACHER'S NOTE:

Some have tried to make a sharp distinction between the agent and agency. They argue that if there is not a distinction within the affirmative case between the two, the affirmative should automatically lose the round. However, most debate coaches do not see any distinction between the agent and the agency. Because they are essentially the same thing, there shouldn't be a big discussion over the need to separate them. The key question to ask someone who insists on separating them is this: What will the separation change?

b) Mandates—The specifics of the change being made to the present system.

c) Funding—Any funding that is necessary to implement the plan.

TEACHER'S NOTE:

Funding can be difficult because the.sources of the funding may not necessarily stem from the resolution. If the affirmative decides to cut a governmental program that has nothing to do with the resolution, it may do so in order to fund the plan. If your debaters decide to do this, though, be aware that the negative will provide the disadvantages of cutting a governmental program. Any nonresolutional means of funding is extratopical and is legitimate as a means of implementing the affirmative case. However, any benefits that stem from the extratopical funding (such as the benefits of cutting a wasteful government program) are illegitimate. See Chapter 8.

d) Enforcement—The branch of government or method that will enforce the plan if necessary.

TEACHER'S NOTE:

Enforcement is probably the most straightforward plan plank because it simply outlines who will ensure that the plan is carried out once it is enacted.

e) Addendum—The right to clarify the plan in further speeches.

II. CASE STRUCTURE STYLES

A. Plan-meet-need case

This structure is the most common and is good for clearly identifying the harms of the current system and the need for change. The plan-meet-need case is a good choice for both advanced and beginning debaters.

1. Harms—This case type identifies significant harms that are inherent within the present system and provides the reason to change that system.

2. Advantages—The advantages help satisfy the stock issue of solvency by showing that the plan would solve the harms of the present system.

B. Comparative advantage case

This case type is useful for comparing the big picture of the present system with the big picture of the affirmative case. The affirmative argues that its case provides significant advantages over the present system that cannot be accomplished in any way other than through adoption of the affirmative plan. Advantages are structured to show significance, inherence/uniqueness, and impact.

C. Goals criteria case

The goals criteria case focuses on certain desirable goals in order to show that the present system is failing to meet those goals and that the affirmative plan would achieve those goals. This type of case structure is most useful when it is easy to identify the intended goals of the present system or governmental program. Affirmatives must thoroughly research the topic to identify clear goals in order to effectively use this case structure.

D. Alternative justification case

This case type is generally considered the weakest of the policy cases. Because the alternative justification case is structured to contain two or more independent minicases that can follow the structure of any of the previous three case types, the affirmative often finds it difficult to sufficiently develop the stock issues in any minicase within the eight-minute 1AC. The advantage of the alternative justification case is that if the negative defeats one minicase, the affirmative can win based on another minicase that contains all of the stock issues.

10 Constructing the Negative Case

OUTLINE

The negative is the most challenging side in debate, requiring the debater to present both on-case and off-case arguments against the affirmative.

TEACHER'S NOTES:

▷ Most of your beginning debaters will be very intimidated at the thought of debating the negative side because of their uncertainty about how to respond to a specific affirmative case. Emphasize that although the negative side is indeed more challenging, the key is preparation. Gathering evidence, thinking, and gathering still more evidence will give your students the confidence they need to successfully refute the affirmative opposition.

▷ Understanding the difference between on- and off-case arguments will help your debaters automatically place what they need to know into distinct categories that can be easily remembered as they argue against the affirmative. Make absolutely sure your debaters understand the difference between these two kinds of arguments before moving on to the rest of the chapter.

On-case arguments are made in response to specific points of an affirmative case, whereas off-case arguments are more general in nature and can usually be run against many different cases. You can explain the difference between the two types of arguments thus: "On-case arguments directly refute the affirmative; off-case arguments relate to the affirmative case but show the negative's perspective."

Although off-case arguments stem from the affirmative case, they are not necessarily specifically related to one particular case point. Instead, off-case arguments address elements of the affirmative case as a whole. The first off-case argument that you should help your students develop is the advantages of the current system, which show that the current system is doing a good job. This negative perspective is essential for proving to the audience that the current system should be upheld.

DISCUSSION QUESTION:

What is the difference between on-case and off-case arguments? *(On-case arguments answer specific points in an affirmative case, whereas off-case arguments provide a general response to elements of the affirmative case from the negative's perspective.)*

I. CONSTRUCTING A NEGATIVE PHILOSOPHY

The negative philosophy explains both the negative's interpretation of the resolution and the specific negative expectations of the affirmative team.

TEACHER'S NOTES:

▷ Unfortunately, some coaches teach the "element of surprise" as the best way to attack the affirmative case. Although this tactic may be beneficial at times, the best debates occur when both teams place all of their expectations and analyses at the beginning of the debate. Negatives should be specific about what they expect of the affirmative team and let everyone know how they are approaching the resolution. This strategy will create a much more focused debate, making it a better educational experience for all involved. Presenting their philosophy in the first speech gives negatives the opportunity to develop their arguments fully.

▷ The negative team's on-case arguments should always relate back to the negative philosophy, showing how the affirmative has not proven what it needs to prove. Off-case arguments should complement the negative philosophy, demonstrating that the current system is working well and offers more benefits than the affirmative plan.

▷ The outline of the 1NC should be drafted before the debate round and should include the following elements: the negative's interpretation of the resolution, the requirements that the negative expects from the affirmative, the overall negative theme for the round, and the negative's specific response to the affirmative case. The first two elements can be written in advance; the last two elements will need to be adapted to the particular affirmative case faced in the round. Negatives will want to draft blocks against anticipated affirmative arguments and know what various themes might be adopted against different types of cases. Then, in the round, negatives can pull from the prepared blocks and themes those that best work against the affirmative case.

A. Offering an alternative view

There are no cookie-cutter approaches to constructing the negative case. Always, though, your debaters should have one foot firmly planted in refutation of the affirmative case and the other firmly planted in defense of the current system. Also, they should always keep in mind that the goal of the negative case is to offer an alternative view, not simply an opposing one.

TEACHER'S NOTES:

▷ Except when running a counterplan, the negative is the defender of the current system and as such should remain focused on presenting "the other side" of the argument. Otherwise, the audience knows only about the bad things the current system is doing.

▷ Encourage your debaters to remember that no system is perfect. Since we are finite humans, we cannot have the perfect knowledge that God has. Consequently, the values we hold and the policies we construct are imperfect. Rather than advocating a perfect policy, the job of the debater is to advocate the best choice for this resolution. Remind negatives that the affirmative plan never exists outside of the context of the resolution.

Offering an alternative view will help your students see the bigger picture of how the affirmative case fits into the context of the current system. Seeing this bigger picture enables them to understand the shortcomings of the current system and to determine whether or not the affirmative is justified in suggesting change.

▷ Off-case arguments are essential for showing an alternative view. After all, how can an audience know whether or not to eliminate the current system if they are not aware of what it is doing well? Without knowing what it is doing well, the only information about the current system the audience has is what the affirmative is presenting. Since the affirmative wants change, the problems it points out will usually be the most extreme problems. By pointing out that these problems need to be put in a larger context, the negative enables the audience to see that the problems are not significant enough to warrant change.

▷ In providing an alternative view, it is good to have the speaker who focuses on the harms be the one to talk about the advantages of the current system—usually the first negative speaker. The 1NC should explain what the current system is doing well in order to overcome the psychological impact of the affirmative harms. Make sure to teach your debaters to specifically refute the affirmative harms as well as present advantages of the current system. In their defense of the current system, they cannot forget to explain why the affirmative case is wrong.

DISCUSSION QUESTION:

What is the difference between offering an opposing view and offering an alternative view? *(An opposing view is negative and only attacks the other team's arguments. An alternative view, on the other hand, is both positive and negative—it attacks the other team's arguments but also constructs positive arguments in favor of an alternative position.)*

B. Addressing the appropriate stock issues

After first offering a brief overview of the negative philosophy by presenting an alternative view, the negative should focus on the most vulnerable stock issues in the affirmative case.

Every argument that the negative team makes should be viewed through the lens of the negative philosophy, that is, through its overall view of the resolution. One purpose of the negative philosophy is to outline the negative team's view of the standards the affirmative must meet in order to fulfill the stock issues. Without the focus of a negative philosophy, the negative case is often disorganized and hard to follow. All stock issue arguments should be clearly related back to the negative philosophy.

TEACHER'S NOTE:

Debate is a very complex activity. There are multiple arguments debaters can make at any given time, requiring them to make tough choices about which argument is best in a particular situation. Beginning debaters often want you to tell them what argument they should make. Obviously, though, you cannot teach your debaters how to respond to every possible argument. Instead, guide them in learning to think for themselves by constantly asking them questions: *How? Why? So what? What do you think?* Keep reminding them of the goal of the negative, the strategies of refutation, and the levels of analysis. Be patient when waiting for your debaters to come up with arguments. This process takes time and cannot be rushed. Remember that your job is to teach them to think for themselves instead of telling them what to think.

At times, however, it may be good to take an affirmative case and critique it for your debaters so they understand where to begin. Or, it may be helpful to have them watch you construct an argument. Such occasions should be the exception, though, not the rule.

Knowing that your job is to teach your students to think should free you from feeling like you need to have all the answers. Every debater I (Jeff) coach knows far more about the topic than I do. My job isn't to give them the most up-to-date information about the topic but to get them asking the right questions that will fill in the holes of the research they are doing. You can best help your debaters by serving as a questioning critic.

FOR FURTHER STUDY:

There is no standard format for the 1NC. If you are not familiar with a format, this example is a good starting point.

Sample 1NC with Negative Philosophy

*Resolved: That the United States should
substantially decrease its dependence on foreign oil.*

Assume that the affirmative case advocates a mandatory switch to hydrogen fuel cell vehicles by the year 2015. In its outline for the 1NC, the negative could incorporate the negative philosophy as follows:

I. Theme & View of Resolution—The negative offers both a theme through which the negative will be arguing against the resolution and a rationale for why the negative position is the better way to view the resolution.

With this case, the negative philosophy could be "balance." The negative team would present evidence to show that balance should be the standard for the round and that the current system achieves a good balance between the reality that current technologies aren't ready for a drastic/immediate switch and the dream of what many are referring to as a "hydrogen economy" where all of our energy is from hydrogen. Many experts think either that hydrogen is "science fiction" or that it will take fifty years until the technology is adequate and the infrastructure is in place. The negative would go on to argue that the affirmative plan does not achieve balance because it places all its hope in hydrogen, taking research monies away from other potential energy solutions.

II. Affirmative Requirements—The negative then goes on to show what standards the affirmative must meet in order to win the debate round. Those standards should make reference to (1) absolute voting issues, (2) stock issues, (3) definitional standards, and/or (4) the negative view of the resolution.

Negatives will want to exegete the wording of the resolution, drawing out key words that influence the context and meaning of the definition. They should pay close attention to words like *substantially* and *significantly*. With this case, negatives would outline what they believe the affirmative team will have to do in order to "substantially" reduce U.S. dependence on foreign oil.

III. Violations—The negative argues that the affirmative has not met the necessary requirements. This part of the speech is where negatives would make specific stock issue arguments and refute specific points of the affirmative case.

II. USING ON-CASE ARGUMENTS

An on-case argument is an argument that directly refutes a point of the affirmative case. On-case arguments are important because they are the common ground upon which the negative will establish its position.

TEACHER'S NOTES:

▷ All of the arguments that are included in a point-by-point refutation are called *on-case arguments*. On-case arguments are literally "on the affirmative case." When a debater says that he is going "down the affirmative case," he is simply stating that he is going to provide point-by-point refutation of the affirmative case.

▷ On-case arguments should be the primary concern of the negative team. Without refuting the affirmative case, the negative has not fulfilled its burden of rejoinder and has therefore allowed for an easy affirmative win. It is true that using both on- and off-case arguments is preferable, but help your students master on-case arguments before moving to off-case arguments.

EXERCISE:

Read an affirmative harm or advantage and require your debaters to refute each point with evidence. Once they are used to going point-by-point, have them use the four strategies of refutation to determine which strategy would be best for each point. Don't allow them to use the same refutation strategy for each point; even if one strategy might work well for each point, teach them to consider the other strategies.

A. Analyzing the affirmative case

Negatives should use the four levels of analysis to help them identify the best lines of attack against the affirmative case. The four levels are in the form of questions that the debater should ask himself as he is analyzing his opponent's arguments.

TEACHER'S NOTE:

The four levels of analysis can be applied to any negative or affirmative speech after the 1AC. The four levels will take on slightly different forms depending upon whether the debater is affirmative or negative, but the principles can be universally applied.

1. Does the evidence support the point? Debaters should make sure that the evidence actually proves the claims of their opponent. See Chapter 3 for tests of evidence.

TEACHER'S NOTE:

Teach your students to listen to the nuances of evidence. Most of the time, evidence will contain qualifier words such as *most, all, some, probably, certainly, never,* or *could.* These words are crucial because they tell us the strength of an author's claim. If a piece of evidence stated, "Eating genetically modified food may lead to an immunity to antibiotics," your students would want to point out that it *may* lead to an immunity of antibiotics. The word *may* tells us how confident the author is.

EXERCISE:

Read a paragraph from a newspaper aloud and have your students paraphrase what you just read. Point out the qualifying words that were used: "Notice that I just said it *may* lead to an immunity, not that it *will* lead to an immunity." Repeat this exercise frequently to help your students become better listeners. A good way to determine how well they listen is to look at how well they take notes during a debate round or in class. Sometimes students may just not know what is important to write down; however, many times students do not take notes because they don't know how to listen. Good listening skills are necessary to good debate skills.

2. Does the point support the harm or the advantage? This level helps debaters analyze the stock issues of inherence and significance.

3. Does the plan solve the harm or produce the advantage? The stock issue of solvency is covered by this level of analysis.

4. Does the case uphold the resolution? This fourth level of analysis answers the question of whether the affirmative has presented a topical, prima facie case.

TEACHER'S NOTE:

These last three levels of analysis—a bit trickier than the first—help debaters understand how their opponent's arguments fit together. To that end, continue to ask the questions *how, why,* and *so what* to encourage your debaters to critically analyze all of the components of an argument. When students grasp the concept of a big-picture view of arguments, their ability to cross-examine opponents and to refute an affirmative case will improve remarkably.

B. Refuting specific case structures

1. Plan-meet-need—This type of case often overstates the problems of the current system. Negatives should show that the affirmative view of the current system is unreasonable, should attack the affirmative advantages, and should show that the affirmative plan would not achieve good results.

2. Comparative advantage—Negatives should focus on proving that the current system is more desirable overall than the affirmative plan by explaining that the negative view of the resolution is the best and by showing that the affirmative case does not uphold this view. Having a negative philosophy will greatly help refutation of a comparative advantage case.

3. Goals criteria—With this case type, negatives should concentrate on the affirmative's goal either by showing how the present system upholds the goal or by demonstrating that the affirmative misunderstands the best goal for the situation.

4. Alternative justification—Negatives are sometimes intimidated by this case structure, but alternative justification cases are usually easy to refute simply by showing how the stock issues are not sufficiently developed in any of the minicases or by pointing out how the minicases contradict one another.

III. USING OFF-CASE ARGUMENTS

Off-case arguments provide additional reasons to reject the affirmative case. The purpose of off-case arguments is to show the complexity of the resolution and expose what the affirmative is attempting to conceal. These goals are achieved primarily by advocating the advantages of the current system and the disadvantages of the affirmative plan, although negatives sometimes choose to give minor repairs or a counterplan as an alternative way to fix the problems.

A. Advantages of the current system

Negatives should give the audience reasons to keep the current system by demonstrating what it is doing well. Advantages are important because they diminish the psychological impact of any harms of the affirmative case.

TEACHER'S NOTE:

Each advantage generally has only one piece of evidence to support it. Because there is time to read only three to five advantages, they must be selectively chosen. Teach your debaters to select the ones that will make the greatest impact: those that most directly relate to the harms/failures of the affirmative case and those that best persuade you. If the evidence supporting an advantage doesn't persuade you, it won't persuade the audience.

B. Disadvantages of the affirmative plan

A disadvantage is a negative consequence of enacting an affirmative plan. Disadvantages help the audience understand that the plan is not as good as the affirmative team is suggesting.

TEACHER'S NOTES:

▷ Because audiences are easily confused by the two different types of disadvantages (harms of eliminating the current system and the harmful effects of the affirmative plan), instruct your debaters to use the term *disadvantages* only when referring to the harmful effects of the affirmative plan. Debaters can indirectly address the harms of eliminating the current system when they advocate the advantages present in that system.

▷ Teach your students to compare the disadvantages of the affirmative plan with the advantages of the current system. By making this comparison, the audience will be able to see the impact of choosing either policy and make an informed decision.

▷ Disadvantages are considered off-case arguments because they do not refute specific points of the affirmative plan but instead focus on the "what if" scenario. The "what if" scenario (sometimes referred to as *post-fiat*) asks the audience to assume that the plan will be enacted, then gives several reasons why enacting the plan would create disadvantages. Until they have attended a few tournaments, debaters usually won't be familiar enough with the plans being run in the league to focus on the "what if" scenario. After several tournaments, however, debaters should easily be able to come up with disadvantages for any affirmative plan.

▷ Make sure that your debaters include link, uniqueness, and impact in each disadvantage. Disadvantage arguments must be as well developed as affirmative harm contentions would be.

▷ If one of the negative speakers focuses on the affirmative harms and the advantages of the current system, the other—generally the second negative speaker—should focus on the plan and advantages of the affirmative case and the disadvantages of enacting the affirmative plan. However, keep in mind that the negative *must address all of the stock issues in the 1NC* in order to fulfill its burden of rejoinder. See the notes from Chapter 6.

EXERCISE:

Assign each team to write negative disadvantages against its own affirmative plan. You can also discuss the various cases being used in your club and either conduct an in-class discussion of likely disadvantages or assign students to write at least one disadvantage of each case.

C. Minor repairs

A minor repair is a small change that eliminates the significant harm of the affirmative case without making a major structural change to the current system. The focus of a minor-repairs argument is to show that the harms are not inherent in the current system since it will take only a minor repair to fix those harms.

TEACHER'S NOTES:

▷ The biggest confusion concerning minor repairs is what constitutes a "minor" repair. The general rule is that if a structural or attitudinal change needs to be made, it is a major repair (counterplan or affirmative plan). A minor repair is easily implemented because it is such a small repair that it would not be contested.

▷ When your students argue a minor repair, there should be no doubt in the mind of either the affirmative team or the audience that they are offering a minor repair. I have been in many rounds where the negative team said, "We could fix the problem by . . ." Such a statement implies that the negative team is simply thinking aloud, brainstorming one of numerous ways the problem could be fixed. Your debaters need to be specific and state, "We are offering a minor repair of . . ." The affirmative team and the audience will then know that the negatives are indeed offering an alternative way to fix the problem.

▷ Some think that offering a minor repair is risky because it is an admission that the harm exists. Although admitting that the harm exists is part of offering a minor repair, the main focus of a minor repair is showing that the affirmative's harm isn't significant. In effect, the negative is saying, "Since this harm can be solved with a minor repair, the harm must not be that significant."

D. Counterplans

The negative counterplan is an off-case argument that offers a competitive option for solving the harms that the affirmative claims exist. Ultimately, counterplans agree that the harms exist but question how to fix them and whether or not the advantages can be gained through implementation of the affirmative plan.

TEACHER'S NOTE:

A negative counterplan looks much like an affirmative plan, with the same basic elements of agency, mandates, funding, and enforcement.

1. Guidelines for running counterplans

a) Counterplans must solve the problems identified in the affirmative case—The purpose of the counterplan is to offer an alternative way to fix the major problem identified in the affirmative case.

TEACHER'S NOTE:

Be careful when allowing your debaters to use this strategy. Counterplans are very difficult to run and are often unsuccessful with an inexperienced judge. Since a counterplan admits that a significant harm exists within the current system, the negative gives up its normal presumption. Thus, the negative assumes a burden of proof (similar to the affirmative's) to offer a prima facie case to solve the problems of the current system. The focus of the debate then becomes the best way to fix the harm.

b) Counterplans must be nontopical—Counterplans should either be mutually exclusive of the affirmative case or be completely outside of the area defined by the resolution.

TEACHER'S NOTE:

Counterplans must be nontopical; however, there is disagreement within the debate community regarding what it means to be nontopical. Consider the two main views: the counterplan is nontopical (1) because the agent of change is different from the agent outlined in the resolution or (2) because the counterplan is different from the affirmative plan. The second view is the most controversial because the counterplan may *seem* topical at first, but when compared with the affirmative plan, is not. When the negative argues that anything falling outside the purview of the affirmative's definitions is nontopical, it is arguing what is called *parametrics*.

2. Fiat power for counterplans—The negative assumes some level of fiat power in order to implement its plan and move the debate toward a substantive clash over which plan would, if enacted, be better.

TEACHER'S NOTE:

Fiat power for a counterplan is very tricky. There are no clear rules about what the negative is allowed to fiat. Most debate scholars simply say that negative fiat must be reasonable. But the question of what is "reasonable" is unclear. For the purposes of a good debate, the negative needs fiat power in order to implement its counterplan. To allow the negative enough room to offer a counterplan, the affirmative should not be incredibly picky about what the negative can and cannot fiat. If the negative fiats numerous organizations at very different levels (the UN, the governments of numerous countries, etc.) it is probably being abusive in its use of negative fiat power.

3. Types of counterplans—This text reviews two broad categories of counterplans.

    a) Mutually exclusive counterplans—This type of counterplan cannot exist at the same time as the affirmative case; it would be impossible to adopt both plans at the same time.

    b) Net-benefit counterplans—This type of counterplan is similar to a comparative advantages case. The negative argues that the counterplan would produce more benefits than the affirmative plan.

11 Value Hierarchies: A Summary of Value Conflicts

OUTLINE

I. THE IMPORTANCE OF VALUES IN SOCIETY

What we value determines how we act and therefore determines the state of society. We must carefully choose our values in order to make sure that our actions uphold godly values and influence the world for good.

II. VALUES CLARIFICATION IN ACADEMIC DEBATE: WEIGHING VALUES

Individuals in society hold values that they use to make judgments about how they will live their lives. People must often choose between two values or two good things. An understanding of how values have been categorized helps with this process.

Terminal values are the values that represent the end state that people strive toward. "Peace" and "beauty" and "national security" are examples of terminal values.

Instrumental values are values that operate as the means to help achieve the terminal values. If the terminal value is "national security," an instrumental value of "a strong defense" would be an instrumental value that would help achieve national security.

Terminal values are the end state; thus, the only value that could be superior to a terminal value would be another terminal value. Instrumental values, however, can be superseded both by other instrumental values and by terminal values. Terminal values are more often used in debate rounds, so debaters should be encouraged to use terminal values whenever they can in their cases.

TEACHER'S NOTES:

▷ In addition to terminal and instrumental values, a third category of values is *core values*. Core values are the values that are most important to us and best define who we are as individuals. Our identities are often related to core values. In other words, to change one of these values would change how we think about ourselves. A terminal value will not necessarily be a core value but will instead be based upon a core value. For example, the terminal value of "life" is based upon the core value of a Christian's "belief in God." Christian debaters should advocate values that are in line with their core beliefs.

▷ The value debate proposition asks us to consider a matter of values and to determine how to use value systems we hold in common to make decisions about what action is most desirable. Because competing values can sometimes be mutually exclusive—seeking "wisdom" and "an exciting life" simultaneously may be impossible—we establish value hierarchies in order to decide how to decide between competing values. The value hierarchy can differ according to the advocate or according to the situation. Is "life" more important than "freedom?" Whose life, and whose freedom?

▷ The value hierarchy often becomes a contested issue of the debate. Both debaters may agree on the terminal value—life—but disagree about how to preserve it: through decreased use of pesticides, or through the use of fertilizers that increase crop yield? Michael Bartanen and David Frank explain that debaters most often present their choice of value hierarchy, link it to the status quo, then attack the value hierarchy of the other team.[1] In this way, part of the debate revolves around which is "the highest value of the round." The side that wins this argument wins much of the strategic ground of the debate.

EXERCISE:

Have students obtain a copy of an opinion of a newspaper editor or a videotape of an editorial opinion from a televised news program. Topics can be international, national, state, regional, or completely local. (Another variation is to pass out some pieces that you have collected from various newspapers or magazines to better control the quality and significance of the material.) Working individually or with a partner, students can then do a values-based analysis of the opinion by completing the following steps:

1. Identify the primary and secondary values upon which the editor is basing his or her opinion.
2. Name the values of the opposing side that are set up and attacked by the editor.
3. Determine if there were other significant values on either side of the controversy that were left out.
4. Declare your own views on the matter in dispute and defend those views by assigning your own value hierarchies to the issue.

To encourage a greater comfort level with values analysis and a greater familiarity with current events, this exercise might be a recurring assignment due every few weeks.

DISCUSSION QUESTION:

What is the difference between a terminal value and an instrumental value? (Instrumental values are a means to an end; terminal values are an end unto themselves.)

III. VALUES HIERARCHIES AT WORK IN THE REAL WORLD: THE ABORTION CONTROVERSY

Our society's debate of the abortion controversy provides an excellent example of how to use value hierarchies in real life. If "life" is the highest value, a common-sense analysis of abortion would conclude that the procedure is wrong because it takes the life of an unborn child. If "freedom of choice" is the highest value, then one could conclude that the right to abortion should be preserved. Or, if "economic well-being" is the highest value, one might conclude that poor women should have the right to abort children they cannot afford.

When a critical thinker places these values in juxtaposition with one another, it becomes very difficult to justify any value other than life. A Christian thinker would certainly have to conclude that the life of the unborn is the highest value that must be upheld in the context of abortion.

EXERCISES:

▷ *My Favorite Restaurant.* Have each person in the room state his favorite restaurant in a city or area with which everyone in the group is familiar. Next, ask each person to give two values that guided his selection. Such values might include affordability, proximity, hours of operation, quality of food, taste, healthiness of food, diversity of food offerings, quickness and/or quality of service, or ambiance. Finally, allow general arguments from the floor appealing to the group's shared values with the purpose of bringing everyone to a common opinion. A vote should then be taken, and if possible, the group should then go there to eat after practice.

This is actually a very practical exercise. As a debate coach who is often on the road with the debate team for weekend tournaments, I (Skip) found that one of the biggest conflicts we had for years was deciding where the team should go to eat. But when we took into consideration what the group's shared values were, it became easier to find an agreeable solution. Our team tended to value quick, affordable places with a diverse menu over greasy, fast-food options or even nicer but slower and more expensive restaurants.

▷ *Real-life Values.* First, have each of your students write down a list of people and things that influence her. This list might include parents, friends, God, television, music, news, and the Internet. Second, have each student rank the items on her list according to who or what has the most influence. Third, have each write down a sentence or two about why each thing influences her. Fourth, break your students up into groups to discuss why they think the things listed on their papers influence them. Fifth, discuss as an entire group what influences society, coming up with a list of the top five. Students will likely be more honest about what influences them if you assure them that the papers need not be turned in.

Outline 11 Endnotes

[1] Michael D. Bartanen and David A. Frank, *Nonpolicy Debate*, 2d ed. (Scottsdale, AZ: Gorsuch Scarisbrick, 1994).

[2] Ibid., 32–34.

12 Constructing Value Cases

I. DEFINING VALUE DEBATE

Value debate focuses argumentation upon the presuppositions underlying political, moral, social, or religious beliefs that would lead to a particular policy decision. Value cases do not, however, advocate a policy. Because beliefs exist within the context of real-life situations, the value case illustrates the value by giving a conflict scenario where a clash of values has occurred or is occurring.

II. Benefits of Value Debate

Among other things, this discipline:

▷ inspires a broadening of knowledge.

▷ grants extensive training in the skill of reasoning.

▷ furnishes practice in the art of persuasion.

▷ teaches consideration of all sides of an argument.

▷ encourages an understanding and strengthening of personal beliefs.

▷ promotes value-based conclusions.

▷ provides exposure to many different worldviews and philosophies.

▷ offers practice with answering other views and defending personal beliefs in an appropriate, non-accusatory manner.

TEACHER'S NOTE:

Of course, the greatest benefit that value debate offers the Christian student is the opportunity to defend and refine a value structure consistent with the Christian faith. Value debate helps students to begin to understand the core beliefs that underlie their own decisions as well as the decisions of others. This skill is invaluable for teaching Christian students how to engage their world for Christ.

III. THE VALUE RESOLUTION

Value resolutions are commonly worded to create a conflict scenario between two desirable values or to create a conflict scenario in which the debater affirms or denies a moralistic claim.

DISCUSSION QUESTION:

Is value debate morally relativistic? *(Value debate is not morally relativistic because it does not force students to advocate the idea that moral absolutes do not exist. Value debate focuses on the application of a value to a particular situation, not the absolute importance of the value. In other words, although the conflict scenario may change which value best applies to a certain situation, the absolute importance of the value itself does not change.)*

IV. THE LINCOLN-DOUGLAS FORMAT

LD debate is named after the memorable political debates between Abraham Lincoln and Stephen Douglas. Questions of value were always a part of these debates. LD debate is therefore a debate between two individuals instead of two teams. The time schedule and format are somewhat different from the schedule followed for team debate.

V. CONSTRUCTING AN AFFIRMATIVE VALUE CASE

As in policy debate, the affirmative must present a topical, prima facie case that fulfills the stock issues. To accomplish this goal, the affirmative should define the important terms of the resolution, offer a value and criterion, and present contentions that show the real-world impacts of the value being either violated or upheld. See Chapter 6 for more on value stock issues.

A. Definitive stock issues: definitions and criteria

1. Definitions—Definitions provide context for the debate. Debaters should clarify key terms in the resolution and any other important terms related to the value or criterion. Definitions are especially important in value debate because of the relative nature of the activity. Definitions provide the common ground for the round.

2. Criteria—The criteria is composed of a value and a criterion.

a) The function and role of the value—The value functions as the standard of measurement by which the topic is evaluated. It is a tangible way of showing benefit to individuals or society. The resolution is viewed through the context of the value.

TEACHER'S NOTE:

Our values influence the conclusions that we draw from evidence. For example, if a piece of evidence reports that the majority of African-Americans between the ages of 25 and 40 are in favor of school vouchers, different people could draw very different conclusions, depending upon their values. One person might value equal opportunity and conclude that school vouchers are desirable. Another might value the public school system and conclude that vouchers are a threat to the economic viability of public schools since parents would be allowed to place their children in private schools at public expense.

EXERCISES:

▷ Have your students analyze this resolution: *Resolved: That the American judicial system has overemphasized freedom of expression.* Have them suggest a value or values that would serve as the context for convincing an audience of the truth of this statement.

▷ Choose an opinion article or editorial that discusses a controversial contemporary issue in terms of values that should be considered in relation to the issue. Have students read the article and locate the values that are used to support the arguments. Ask students questions such as these:

▷▷ *What forms of evidence does the author offer for his arguments?*

▷▷ *What values does he hold?*

▷▷ *What values does he think his audience holds?*

▷▷ *Suppose the author was addressing homeschool debate judges. Would his arguments change? How?*

▷▷ *What is the overall quality of the author's evidence and reasoning?*

b) The function and role of the criterion—The criterion is the key definitive stock issue. It is the standard by which the value is measured.

TEACHER'S NOTES:

▷ The chosen criterion determines how the rest of the debate can be argued. For instance, with the resolution *Resolved: That the United States is justified in providing military support to nondemocratic countries,* the arguments supporting the resolution would differ using the value of freedom as opposed to the value of order.

▷ A sample list of values and criterions is given at the end of this chapter outline.

EXERCISE:

Choose several values familiar to the students in your group. Have the students list several different criterions that could be used to determine whether the value is being met or is being violated.

B. Designative stock issues: correspondence and application

The affirmative must show the application and relevance of the value to the real world by offering contentions that illustrate a conflict scenario in which the affirmative value is being either violated or upheld. In doing so, the affirmative must be sure that there is correspondence between its definitions, its criteria, and its contentions. In other words, the value and criterion defined in the first part of the case must be the same value and criterion illustrated in the contentions.

VI. USING EVIDENCE EFFECTIVELY

The relationship between the resolution, the criteria, and the real-world example must be established with evidence. Value debaters use two general types of evidence: (1) evidence that defines, explains, and prioritizes the value and the criterion (usually philosophical in nature); and (2) evidence that illustrates the real-world contentions (generally from current events sources).

TEACHER'S NOTES:

▷ Keeping a file of values and the arguments made to support those values will help you as you coach teams in future years.

▷ Value debate may require less evidence than policy debate, but evidence still plays an essential role in establishing value arguments. Evidence is necessary to prove that a debater's value-criterion is the highest in the round, to show how the value is being violated in the current system, and to prove the real-world impact of the violation.

Values and criterions are often interchangeable. The following lists distinguish between those that are most commonly used as values, those that are most commonly used as criterions, and those that can be used as either. The use of values and criterions is completely dependent on the conflict scenario being debated. Therefore, these lists should be seen not as concrete categories that must be adhered to in a debate, but rather as general categories intended to guide understanding of the possibilities for values and criterions.

Values

Democracy
Equality
Freedom
Justice
Liberty
Life
Morality
Nature
Peace
Safety
Sanctity of Life
Social Cohesion
Truth
Unity

Criterions

Circumstantial Evaluation
Cooperation
Cost Benefit Analysis
Fairness
Net Benefits

Either

Communitarianism
Compassion
Dialogue
Diplomacy
Humanitarianism
Individualism
Pragmatism
Privacy
Quality of Life
Security
▷ Economic
▷ Family
▷ Future
▷ National
▷ Personal
▷ Physical
Social Contract
Utilitarianism
Veracity

13 Value Debate: Approaching the Affirmative and Negative

I. GENERAL APPROACHES

A. Better versus best

Beginning debaters often see things in a sharp dichotomy of good and bad. However, value resolutions are usually constructed in a way that requires debaters to argue between two good values. In these situations, the debater must argue that one value is best rather than argue that his opponent's value is absolutely wrong.

B. Degrees, not extremes

There is no need to eliminate one value in favor of another (extremes); instead, debaters should merely elevate one value above another (degrees).

C. Reasoning over evidence

A value debater should focus on reasoning more than on evidence. It is reasoning that provides the backbone of value debate and guides the use of evidence.

TEACHER'S NOTE:

Reasoning is extremely important since the value debater must focus on the relationship between the criteria and the contentions, yet this emphasis on reasoning does not diminish the importance of evidence. Evidence remains an integral part of value debate.

D. Persuasion, not coercion

Value debaters can focus on persuasion by being sure to emphasize the real-life consequences of the value violation rather than by trying to coerce the audience with emotional appeals that are divorced from substantive truths.

TEACHER'S NOTE:

Any issue where values are emphasized evokes emotion. Emotion cannot be separated from reason because our decisions and judgments take many factors into account, including emotion. Appeals to emotion are abusive, though, if the speaker appeals to emotion alone. The best persuasion is the marriage of reason and emotion. See the *Teacher's Note* regarding pathos in the outline for Chapter 1.

II. APPROACHING THE AFFIRMATIVE VALUE CASE

A. Preparation

Preparation focuses on *how* and *why* questions: Why is this value important to society? How has it been violated or upheld?

1. Research—Debaters can obtain value evidence from philosophical as well as current events sources. Value debate requires research into the value itself, its importance, and its historic place in our society.

TEACHER'S NOTE:

Historic documents that explain the importance of values in American society are very helpful: The Declaration of Independence, the Constitution, the *Federalist Papers*, and other documents written by our Founding Fathers. *Bartlett's Book of Quotations* is also a helpful starting point for value evidence.

2. Construction—As debaters construct their six-minute cases, they should ask themselves the following questions:
▷ *Why is the evidence important?*
▷ *How does the evidence support the value and the criterion?*
▷ *What is the impact of these arguments upon the lives of the audience?*

3. Refinement—Debaters should refine their cases by reading them aloud several times, eliminating unnecessary words and phrases, and carefully checking that every point helps prove the criteria.

B. Practice

Practice tournaments or practice rounds in class are the very best way to strengthen the affirmative case.

1. Necessary and secondary arguments

a) Necessary arguments—Affirmatives must answer negative arguments that directly refute the affirmative case (such as countercriteria or the direct refutation of evidence as it applies to the resolution and the criteria).

b) Secondary arguments—Affirmatives should view negative arguments that question elements of the affirmative case based upon probability as secondary to arguments that directly oppose affirmative criteria or evidence. These are the three most common secondary arguments:

(1) Example—In an attempt to prove that the affirmative *might* be wrong, negatives sometimes try to loosely relate evidence to the affirmative case through hypothetical, extreme, or remote examples that fall outside of the conflict scenario identified by the affirmative.

(2) Alternate cause—The negative argues in abstract terms that there are many possible alternate causes that could affirm the resolution other than the real-life examples given in the affirmative conflict scenario. This type of argument is secondary because the negative is not substantiating any of its claims but merely saying what *might* be the case. Affirmatives should not be distracted by these arguments, but should instead emphasize the reality of the affirmative's conflict scenario.

(3) Analogy—Negatives sometime try to use an analogy, often from history, to show how the affirmative's value or criterion did not work in another situation. Often, these analogies have factors that are very different from the ones present in the affirmative's conflict scenario.

TEACHER'S NOTE:

Teaching debaters the difference between necessary and secondary arguments can be somewhat frustrating because debaters are usually inclined to respond to every single argument brought by their opponents. Although responding to all arguments is a good habit, it is often impossible to do so within the time limits of LD debate.

Secondary arguments are important but are not the primary focus of the debate. The best thing a coach can do is to require that everything the affirmative argues relate to its criteria. If the argument doesn't relate to the criteria, then the argument is secondary.

EXERCISE:

When judging a practice round, require your students to relate all of their arguments to the affirmative criteria. If your debaters are not relating all of their arguments to the criteria, interrupt and ask them *how the argument relates* to help them understand the difference between necessary and secondary arguments.

---

2. Affirmative speeches—For the constructive speech, LD debaters can review the general principles in Chapters 8 and 9 regarding the 1AC and 2AC policy speeches. This chapter focuses on the rebuttal speeches since they are some of the most difficult speeches in academic debate. The affirmative has only seven minutes to refute thirteen minutes of negative argumentation.

a. First affirmative rebuttal—The affirmative should prepare an outline of the essential affirmative arguments in order to maintain proper focus throughout this speech. Debaters can use the cross-examination time to help determine which arguments are essential.

b. Second affirmative rebuttal—The goal of this speech is to affirm the resolution by rebuilding the affirmative case rather than by simply refuting negative arguments.

TEACHER'S NOTE:

The exercises for the 1AR and 2AR in the outline of Chapter 6 will be helpful to use here as well.

III. APPROACHING THE NEGATIVE VALUE CASE

A. Components of the negative case

1. The negative philosophy—The philosophy is an outline of the negative interpretation of the resolution and of the negative arguments against the entire affirmative case. Its purpose is to give the negative a unified means for presenting all of the negative arguments in the round.

2. Countercriteria—Debaters can refute the affirmative's value in one of two ways: by accepting the affirmative value but refuting the affirmative's application of the value, or by offering a countervalue and proving its superiority over the affirmative value. A countervalue is developed much like the affirmative value.

TEACHER'S NOTE:
A sample list of values and criterions is located in the outline of Chapter 12.

3. Point-by-point refutation—Point-by-point refutation of affirmative contentions should be run using the same philosophy advanced against the affirmative value and criterion.

TEACHER'S NOTE:
Negatives can choose to attack the evidence, the argument, or both. They should focus on the weaknesses of the affirmative case, remembering that it is not necessary to argue every point of the affirmative case. It may be wise to concede (1) claims which the affirmative is certain to win, (2) claims that will require the negative to contradict earlier arguments, and (3) claims that enhance negative arguments.

4. Value objections—A value objection is an off-case argument that highlights harms that will occur when the affirmative value is applied to the conflict scenario. Value objections are similar to disadvantages run against a policy case.

B. Negative speeches

1. First negative constructive—There is only one negative constructive speech in LD debate. Therefore, all negative arguments for the round must be presented in this speech. The 1NC should question affirmative evidence, examine the significance of affirmative claims, and determine the extent to which the affirmative has proved its claims. The rebuttal speech may reinforce and extend only these arguments made in this speech, and no others.

TEACHER'S NOTES:

▷ Without knowing when the value violation occurs, the judge does not know how to measure the truth of the resolution. If the affirmative does not clearly explain how to measure the application of the value, the negative should immediately point out this failure to the judge.

▷ All the elements of the stock issues must be present in order for the affirmative to successfully present a logically defensible case. The stock issues are a good way to evaluate an argument but a poor way to decide who wins the value debate round. The negative must offer an alternate view of the resolution, giving the judge an alternative position to consider when making her decision.

EXERCISE:

Help your debaters think through the following questions as you discuss negative strategies:

▷ *Is the source of evidence biased?*
▷ *Does the evidence presented uphold affirmative claims?*
▷ *Does any element of the case contradict the evidence?*
▷ *What is the significance of the affirmative claim?*
▷ *What is the impact of the claim upon the resolution?*
▷ *Does the criterion work to measure the violation of the value?*
▷ *Is there a better value or criterion to measure the truth of the resolution?*

2. First negative rebuttal—The arguments made in the 1NC will be reinforced and expanded in this speech. The rebuttal centers on refuting the central idea of the debate. Negatives should use a cohesive theme that focuses on the negative value or overall philosophy of the round. In the 1NR, the debater should break away from the words of others and use his own rhetorical skills to persuade the audience that his theme makes the most sense. He should be encouraged to use pathos, eye contact, and effective nonverbal communication in his speech delivery.

EXERCISE:

Have students choose a refutation argument from a recent debate practice or tournament and recreate that rebuttal speech for the debate club. After each speech, allow the other members of the team to give constructive input on how each student could improve.

APPENDIX

Team Activities

by David H. Robey

But in fact God has arranged the parts in the body, every one of them, just as he wanted them to be. If they were all one part, where would the body be? As it is, there are many parts, but one body.

—I Corinthians 12:18–20, NIV

Every effective team is comprised of "many members" with highly varied personalities, gifts, and communication styles. For these unique individuals to learn to work together as "one body" is often no easy task!

Engaging your group in team activities can help facilitate the process. The following exercises—many of which are included in the branch of personnel training called *experiential education*—provide opportunities for debaters to learn key lessons about teamwork as they strive to become a unit. It is essential to note that the success of each activity depends not only upon the correct handling of the activity itself but also upon the correct processing of the responses to each activity. The exercises are designed to be physical in nature and emotional in content. Have fun with them!

1. Name That Tune

Goal: To demonstrate various leadership styles by having students hum songs in order to locate the members of a group.

Description of Activity: Print the titles of common songs on slips of paper: "Happy Birthday," "Row-Row-Row Your Boat," "Jingle Bells," "Three Blind Mice," "Mary Had a Little Lamb," etc. Distribute the song titles randomly. In a group of fifteen, you could distribute five different song titles each repeated three times; for a group of fifty, you might want ten groups of five people, so you would use ten song titles repeated five times each.

Instruct the group that the goal is for each of them to find the other people who share their song title. To do so, they are allowed only to hum the tunes of their songs. Explain that they are not allowed to show anyone their slips of paper, mouth words, make hand gestures, or in any way communicate the song titles other than by humming the tunes. After everyone understands, say, "Go." Immediately, the room will be filled with chaos.

After four or five minutes, stop the game and freeze the groups. More than likely some groups will have formed completely, some partially, and some not at all. Perhaps a prize can be given to the first complete group to form.

Process the Game: A question-and-answer format may be used to process this game.

Leader: *How did you feel when you were first given the task?*

Answers: *Silly! Embarrassed! Confused!*

Leader: *Many people given a team task feel this same way. How did you feel when the humming started?*

Answers: *It was so noisy. I couldn't hear what I was listening for. Someone was humming at me loudly and I was humming a different tune back and I could not tell what he or she was humming.*

Leader: *Often in teams, we hear messages that confuse us. We do not like what we are hearing. We can't hear what we want to hear. Often in leadership, the quality of the message is distorted by the delivery of the message. How did you feel when you discovered someone humming your tune?*

Answers: *Very happy! I knew that I was doing something right! It encouraged me to find the rest of the members of my team.*

(It should be noted that often the joining of two soft hummers results in a team of very loud hummers.)

Leader: *Some teams formed quickly and others did not. Why?*

Answers: *Some people are louder hummers! They positioned themselves so that everyone could hear them! They were more outgoing than other hummers!*

Leader: *This is the way with leadership styles. Some are more direct than others but the goal of all leadership is to unite the members of the team.*

2. The Match Game

Goal: To promote honest communication by having each person share "the most important thing in my life" with the other members of his team during the time it takes to burn a paper match.

Description of Activity: Divide the team into groups of four and have each small group arrange itself into a circle. One member of each team (or an adult) strikes a paper match and holds it parallel to the floor over a piece of aluminum foil or other heat resistant object. A paper match will generally burn no more than twenty seconds, so all members will be able to share in under three minutes. As the match burns, one group member quickly tells about the most important thing in his life. Repeat with the other three group members.

Process the Game: This activity profoundly encourages team members to share their hearts. Point out that the audience members tended to stare at the match, which became a type of clock, and not at the eyes of the other members of the group. Thus, the use of the match not only kept the time moving but also helped the group avoid direct eye contact with each other, which is often a barrier to honest communication.

3. Patty-cake

Goal: To demonstrate conflict escalation by having each team member slap the hands of a partner.

Description of Activity: Divide the team into groups of two. It is wise to have men with men and women with women, keeping the physical characteristics of each two-member team as uniform as possible. Have the two members decide which one of them will be Person A and which will be Person B. Then proceed with the game:

> Leader: *The goal of this game is to determine your level of assertiveness. I want you to find a place away from the walls or furniture and face each other with your hands raised to each other as though you were playing "patty-cake." On the count of three, I want Person A to sharply strike the palms of Person B. This is not a hold or a push but just a good solid slap of palms. Person A will slap and Person B will receive. Get ready, get set, go.*

(There is a slap.)

Leader: *I'm not sure all of you understood me. We want the A's to really be assertive. Don't hurt the other person; just give an appropriately solid slap to communicate your assertiveness. This time, really commit yourself to it.* (You will see the B's spreading their foot base, leaning forward, and getting ready to receive the blow without losing their balance.)

Leader: *Get ready, get set, go.*

(There is a slap.)

Leader: *That still wasn't very good. Now, B's, let's show them how it really should be done. Ready, get set, go.*

(There is a slap.)

Process the Game: You might process the game in the following way:

Leader: *Let me ask the A's, how many of you were slapped harder than you slapped?*

(Many of them will say they were slapped harder.)

Leader: *The premise of this exercise is that conflict always escalates. Even when members are on the same team, it is easy to have conflict between members. When anger becomes a part of a conversation, voices get louder, speech gets faster, and emotions get rawer. Unless there is a deliberate strategy, anger will always escalate. One other thing: If I had had the B's all sit down without a chance to hit back at the A's, I would have had a room full of angry B's. In the same way, as we work together you will need to be careful that you don't direct a strong message at a team member without giving him a chance to respond to that message. Communication that is not two-way often ends in conflict. Winning teams need to have a strategy to keep anger from escalating and need to make sure that communication is always two-way.*

4. Talk to the Animals

Goal: To have small groups consider the benefits and liabilities of four different approaches to problem solving, as represented by four animals.

Description of Activity: Place pictures of the following animals in separate corners of the room: lion, fox, chameleon, and turtle. Explain to the group that each of these animals represents a personality style, or a way of getting things done.

Team members can be allowed to choose one of the animals or they can be divided up by counting off ("1, 2, 3, 4") into four groups. After the groups are in place, instruct each team to discuss the characteristics of the assigned animal and then determine what a person with those same characteristics tends to model that is beneficial and that is destructive to communication.

The following chart suggests possible answers:

Animal	Characteristics	Beneficial	Destructive
Lion	Strong Bold Predatory	Focused Self-reliant Independent thinker Stands his ground Undaunted by challenge	Critical—may hurt others Not a team player Naturally stands out
Fox	Smart Sneaky Fast	Confident, winsome Clever Quick thinker	Overconfident, cocky Unpredictable, untrustworthy Self-centered, not a team player
Chameleon	Adaptable/blends in Sensitive to environment Climber/agile Clingy/sticky	Flexible, easy to get along with Skillfully adapts arguments to new audience Verbal and logical agility Sensitive to even non-verbal communication	Sometimes tries to hide or avoid conflict Focused on self-preservation Too willing to compromise Unpredictable
Turtle	Slow Has a long life Hard-shelled	Blends in—does not draw special attention to itself Steady Patient Methodical Thorough Resolute	Thick-skinned—able to withstand stress, pressure Slow to think, process, and respond Quietly stubborn Can be insensitive Withdraws when conflict arises

Process the Game: Have each group share the benefits and liabilities of its animal, perhaps listing them on a chart such as the one above. Share with the team that at different times, both in debate as well as in life, it is important for people to understand the benefits and dangers of any particular role that they play.

5. The Listening Triangle

Goal: To have group members experience the difficulty of truly listening to an emotionally charged message with which one disagrees by engaging in a staged scenario involving a speaker, a listener, and an evaluator.

Description of Activity: Divide your team into groups of three people each. Each group is made up of a *sender* (Person A), a *listener* (Person B), and an *evaluator* (Person C). The trio should be seated so that A and B have direct eye contact with each other and C is off to the side, able to see both people but out of their direct line of sight. Assign each member one of the following tasks:

Person A: This person will send a strong "I feel" message of a controversial nature to Person B. While it is helpful if A really believes what she is advocating, she can assume a position she doesn't really agree with and just play a role. You can have the message-sender select her own message, or you might want to prepare topics in advance and distribute them to the A members. Topics might be along the line of, "I believe that we should have no censorship of violence on television," "I believe that we should eat only natural, organic foods," or "I believe that anyone should be able to own any gun he wants to." The more bold the ideas and statements get, the more difficult it will be for B to listen and not share his own ideas.

Person B: The goal of B is to clearly understand the position of A. He may question for clarification, rephrase what he has heard in his own words, ask for repetition, or use any active-listening tool in order to clearly understand the message sent by A. Emphasize that he is not to approve or disapprove of what is being said. The goal is for him to clearly understand and be able to articulate a message with which he may strongly disagree.

Person C: Determining the extent to which B has heard and understood the message of person A is the purpose of the evaluator. C should evaluate all the communication techniques employed: choice of words, body language, tone of voice, etc. C then shares with the entire group what was learned from viewing this dyad. Often, C will comment that B's body language clearly said he didn't approve of the message. C may also comment on the type of questions B used. Were the questions neutral and used only as an aid to explore the message, or did the questions reveal that B clearly had a personal agenda?

Process the Game: The key to success with the listening triangle is how the experience is processed. After Person C shares his observations with the group, discuss the difficulties and advantages of *really* listening to and understanding an opposing view.